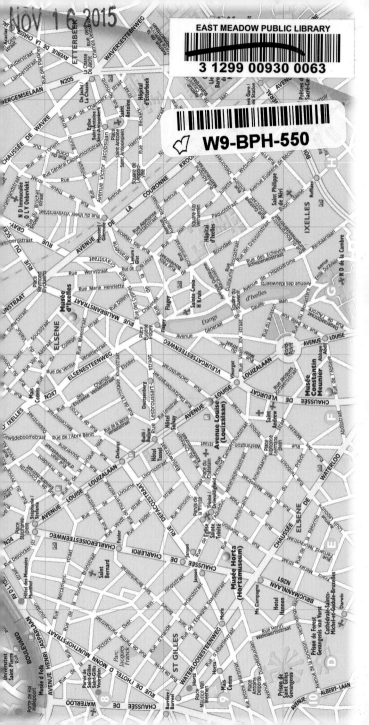

Fodor's
25 Best

BRUSSELS & BRUGES

CHECK FOR
ACCOMPANYING MAP

How to Use This Book

KEY TO SYMBOLS

➕ Map reference to the accompanying fold-out map

✉ Address

☎ Telephone number

🕐 Opening/closing times

🍴 Restaurant or café

🚉 Nearest rail station

Ⓜ Nearest subway (Metro) station

🚌 Nearest bus route

🚢 Nearest riverboat or ferry stop

♿ Facilities for visitors with disabilities

❓ Other practical information

▷ Further information

ℹ Tourist information

✋ Admission charges:
Expensive (more than €8)
Moderate (€4–€8)
Inexpensive (€4 or less)

This guide is divided into four sections
• Essential Brussels and Bruges: An introduction to the cities and tips on making the most of your stay.
• Brussels and Bruges by Area: We've recommended the best sights, shops, entertainment venues, nightlife and restaurants in each city. Suggested walks help you to explore on foot.
• Where to Stay: The best hotels, whether you're looking for luxury, budget or something in between.
• Need to Know: The info you need to make your trip run smoothly, including getting about by public transport, weather tips, emergency phone numbers and useful websites.

Navigation In the Brussels and Bruges by Area chapter, we've given each area its own color, which is also used on the locator maps throughout the book and the map on the inside front cover.

Maps The fold-out map accompanying this book has comprehensive street plans of Brussels and Bruges. The grid on this fold-out map is the same as the grid on the locator maps within the book. We've given grid references within the book for each sight and listing.

Contents

**ESSENTIAL BRUSSELS
AND BRUGES**   **4–18**

Introducing Brussels and
   Bruges   4–5
A Short Stay in Brussels
   and Bruges   6–7
Top 25   8–9
Shopping   10–11
Shopping by Theme   12
Brussels and Bruges
   by Night   13
Eating Out   14
Restaurants by Cuisine   15
Top Tips For…   16–18

**BRUSSELS AND BRUGES
BY AREA**   **19–106**
CENTRAL BRUSSELS   **20–46**

Area Map   22–23
Sights   24–37
Walk   38
Shopping   40–41
Entertainment
   and Nightlife   42–43
Restaurants   44–46

SOUTH BRUSSELS   **47–62**

Area Map   48–49
Sights   50–55
Bicycle Tour   56
Shopping   57–58
Entertainment
   and Nightlife   59
Restaurants   60–62

BRUGES   **63–92**

Area Map   64–65
Sights   66–86
Walk   87
Shopping   88–89
Entertainment
   and Nightlife   90
Restaurants   91–92

FARTHER AFIELD   **93–106**

Area Map   94–95
Sights   96–102
Excursions   103–106

WHERE TO STAY   **107–112**

Introduction   108
Budget Hotels   109
Mid-Range Hotels   110–111
Luxury Hotels   112

NEED TO KNOW   **113–125**

Planning Ahead   114–115
Getting There   116–117
Getting Around   118–119
Essential Facts   120–121
Language   122–123
Timeline   124–125

CONTENTS

Introducing Brussels and Bruges

Brussels and Bruges represent the twin identities of contemporary Belgium. Brussels is the larger, busier city—and Europe's political capital. Bruges, in Flanders, is one of Europe's best-preserved medieval cities and Belgium's tourist capital.

Brussels is a cosmopolitan city: The population was already divided into Flemish and French speakers, but to these are now added the babel of European languages, with English as a common denominator. Speak to anyone who has lived here for a while and they will tell you that it is a very pleasant city to be in, with its wonderful museums, splendid architecture, delightful green spaces, excellent, reasonably priced restaurants and a lively nightlife.

The heart of the city is finally being restored and revitalized. The district around rue Dansaert, close to the Grand' Place, has become a trendy spot to live or hang out in and nearby streets such as rue des Chartreux and chaussée de Flandres regularly see the opening of another hip boutique or restaurant. Other areas are also undergoing a revival, as young European professionals choose to live in the gorgeous art nouveau districts of Ixelles and St.-Gilles rather than in the suburbs.

Bruges attracts more than 2.5 million visitors each year. Flemish is the local language, although most people also know enough English to communicate with visitors. The heart of the city is small and most sights are within walking distance. If you don't want to walk, do as the locals do and go by bicycle. Unlike Brussels, Bruges spent the last decades trying to keep its look medieval. The Concertgebouw, which opened in 2002, was the first statement that contemporary architecture could have a place here. Now there is a desire to create a broader environment where today's artists can be inspired by the city's rich past.

Facts + Figures

- There are a staggering 139 restaurants for every square mile (2.6sq km) in Brussels.
- Bruges was European City of Culture in 2002.
- More than 150 monuments in Bruges have been protected.

BRUSSELS DISTRICTS

The heart of Brussels is enclosed by the "Petit Ring," which more-or-less follows the 14th-century city walls. The Lower Town, near the Grand' Place, is where the working classes lived. Now fashionable, it has great restaurants and bars. The French-speaking upper classes lived, and many still do, on the hill, the Upper Town. This area has a lot of grand buildings.

CITY OF BRIDGES

No name is more appropriate than *Brugge*, Flemish for bridges. The city had its origins by a bridge over the canal *(reie)*, most probably the Blinde Ezelbrug (Blind Donkey Bridge). To protect the crossing, a borough was built around the bridge and the city grew around it. Bruges still counts many canals and about 80 bridges.

CITY OF BUREAUCRATS

Brussels is home not only to the national government of Belgium, but also to the parliaments of two of the country's three regions: Flanders and Brussels (the parliament of Wallonia sits in Namur). It also houses the European parliament and the headquarters of NATO. The European Union employs around 40,000 people in the city.

A Short Stay in Brussels and Bruges

DAY 1 BRUSSELS

Morning Start the day early at the **Grand' Place** (▷ 26), admiring all the superb Gothic facades as well as the tower of the **Hôtel de Ville** (▷ 25). Rub the bronze plaque of Charles Buls, just off the square, for good luck and continue to **Manneken-Pis** (▷ 28). Stroll along **rue Antoine Dansaert** (▷ St.-Géry and Ste.-Catherine, 37) to get familiar with Belgian fashion and stop for some oysters and a glass of white wine from the stall on **place Ste.-Catherine** (▷ 37). Check out the newest space for contemporary art, the **Centrale Électrique** (▷ 35).

Lunch Have a *Bruxellois* lunch at one of the many restaurants on the Chaussée de Flandres, particularly **Viva M'Boma** (▷ 46) or at **Vismet** (▷ 46) for the freshest fish and seafood.

Afternoon Head for the **Sablon** (▷ 34) and enjoy a coffee on a heated terrace, before a serious dip into both old and modern art at the **Musées d'Art Ancien et Moderne** (▷ 29–31), founded by Napoleon in 1801. Browse around in the antiques shops or take in another museum if you can. The wonderful **Musée des Instruments de Musique** (▷ 32) is a good choice—the collection of musical instruments here is one of the most important of its kind in the world and it has great views from its roof terrace. End the afternoon with a stroll through the **Parc de Bruxelles** (▷ 33), once the hunting ground of Belgian kings and now a haven for Bruxellois and visitors alike, with its tree-lined avenues and fountain.

Dinner See the **Grand' Place** (▷ 26) by night, take a walk through the **Galeries Royales St.-Hubert** (▷ 41) and eat in a typical Brussels brasserie: the **Taverne du Passage, Vincent** or the grander **Belga Queen** (▷ all 44–46). After dinner have a nightcap at one of the bars on **place St.-Géry** (▷ 37) or at **l'Archiduc** (▷ 42).

DAY 2 BRUGES

Morning Start the day with a delicious breakfast at one of Bruges' top bakeries, **Servaas Van Mullem** (▷ 89). Walk over to the **Markt** (▷ 76), taking in the impressive Belfry, rising 83m (272ft) above the town. If it is a clear day, climb up for sweeping views over the city and surrounding countryside. Back down again, a narrow street leads to the even more perfect square of **Burg** (▷ 68), with the fine Gothic facade of the **Town Hall** and the **Basiliek Van Het Heilig-Bloed** (▷ 83), where a service for the Adoration of the Holy Blood still takes place every Friday morning. Pass the **Vismarkt** (▷ 86) and walk along de Dijver to the **Groeninge Museum** (▷ 72), with its superb collection of Flemish Primitives.

Lunch Have a typical Belgian lunch at **Den Dyver** (▷ 91), which serves traditional dishes cooked with beer.

Afternoon Continue to the **Begijnhof** (▷ 66) and enjoy the tranquility of the nearby Minnewater (Lovers' Lake). Walk through the small alleys to the old **St.-Janshospitaal** (▷ 80), an interesting building in itself, which houses a fine collection of Hans Memling's paintings. Opposite the medieval hospice rises the large brick tower of the **Onze-Lieve-Vrouwekerk** (▷ 78), with Michelangelo's statue of *Madonna and Child* and other treasures. Stroll through the garden to the **Gruuthuse Museum** (▷ 74) next door. If you have any time left, take a **canal cruise** (▷ 70), starting from just opposite the museum, or ride a *koets* (horse-drawn carriage) through town from the Burg.

Dinner If you reserve well in advance, you can enjoy dinner at **De Karmeliet** (▷ 92), one of Bruges' best restaurants. If not, try the romantic setting of **Chez Olivier** (▷ 91). After dinner, you can work off the calories by strolling along the well-lit canals.

▶ ▶ ▶ BRUSSELS

Centre Belge de la Bande Dessinée ▷ 24
A must-see for comic strip *aficionados*.

Grand' Place ▷ 26–27
Admire the imposing mix of architectural brilliance in Brussels' famous square.

Heysel ▷ 98–99
Home of the 1958 World Exhibition, with its landmark Atomium.

De Vesten en Poorten ▷ 82 These city fortifications have protected Bruges for more than 600 years.

St.-Janshospitaal en Memling Museum ▷ 80–81 Hans Memling's artworks, housed in an ancient hospice.

Onze-Lieve-Vrouwekerk ▷ 78–79
Magnificent 13th-century church with important medieval art.

Markt ▷ 76–77
Since the 13th century this market square has been central to Bruges' activities.

Kathedraal St.-Salvator ▷ 75 A 13th-century place of worship containing sculptures and art.

Gruuthuse Museum ▷ 74 A glorious medieval palace with an interesting museum.

Groeninge Museum ▷ 72–73 Flemish art from the 15th century to today.

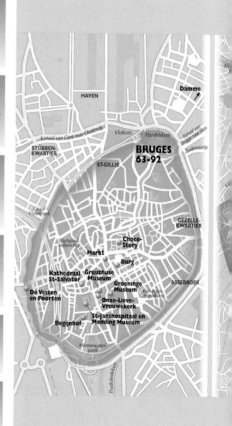

Damme ▷ 96–97 Just 6.5km (4 miles) outside Bruges, this lovely little town is worth a visit.

Choco-Story ▷ 71 Learn all there is to know about chocolate, and then taste the product.

These pages are a quick guide to the Top 25 sights, described in more detail later. Here they are listed alphabetically, starting with the sights in Brussels and followed by those in Bruges. The tinted background shows which area each sight is in.

Hôtel de Ville ▷ 25 Brussels has the most elegant of all Belgium's Gothic town halls.

Jardin Botanique Meise ▷ 100–101 One of the largest botanical gardens in the world.

Manneken-Pis ▷ 28 Brussels' diminutive bronze statue of a small boy continues to draw crowds.

Musée d'Art Ancien ▷ 30–31 Don't miss the classical art housed here.

Musée d'Art Moderne ▷ 29 Home to modern Belgian art.

Musée des Instruments de Musique ▷ 32 See musical instruments from across the globe.

Musée Horta ▷ 52–53 Art nouveau at its absolute best is on show at Victor Horta's former home.

Parc du Cinquantenaire ▷ 50–51 Museums, auto exhibitions and monuments are all here, in one place.

Place Royale ▷ 33 An elegant neoclassical square overlooked by imposing palaces and monuments.

Le Sablon ▷ 34 Sit and people-watch on the terraces of this delightful square.

Heysel (Heizel), Jardin Botanique Meise

BassinVergote Vergotedok

Parc Albert I park

ELBERG

BEEK

Parc Max- miller-park

SCHAERBEEK

CENTRAL BRUSSELS 20–46

Jardin Botanique Kruidtuin Gent

ST JOSSE ST JOOST

TEN NODE

Centre Belge de la Bande Dessinée

Grand' Place (Grote Markt)

Hôtel de Ville

Parc de Bruxelles Park van Brussel

Manneken Pis

Musée des Instruments de Musique

Musée d'Art Moderne

Place Royale

Parc du Cinquantenaire Jubelpark

UTH USSEL -62

BRUSSEL

LE SABLON

Musée d'Art Ancien

Parc Léopold Leopoldspark

LES MAROLLES

Parc d'Egmont Egmontpark

ELSENE

ETTERBEEK

ST GILLIS

Parc Jacques Franck

ST GILLES

Musée Horta (Hortamuseum)

Parc d'Alsace

Parc de Forest Park van Vorst

ELSENE

IXELLES

Cimetière d'Ixelles Begraafplaats van Elsene

EST VORST

BRUSSEL

Bois de la Cambre

Parc Duden park

Parc Brugmann park

Parc Montjoie park

UKKEL

Canal Cruise ▷ 70 A wonderful way to explore the city known as the "Venice of the North."

Burg ▷ 68–69 A medieval square bounded on all sides by impressive buildings of historical note.

Begijnhof ▷ 66–67 This pretty square of houses was home to an all-female pious community.

BRUGES ◀ ◀ ◀

9

Shopping

An obvious souvenir from Belgium, if not a lasting one, is food. Belgium is known for its plain chocolate, which contains only the best cocoa and a very high proportion of it.

A Chocoholic's Dream Destination

Belgians are serious about their chocolate, as is obvious from the number of shops devoted to chocolate in its many shapes, shades and tastes. You can buy good chocolate bars, such as Côte d'Or, in supermarkets, but it's the handmade chocolates and pralines that stand out. Prices are generally low, except for chocolates by the high priest of chocolate, Pierre Marcolini, or by the internationally renowned Godiva (both ▷ 41). Do as the Belgians do and look for smaller patisseries that make their own, including Spegelaere (▷ 89) and Depla Pol (▷ 88) in Bruges and Mary's (▷ 41) in Brussels.

The Way the Cookie Crumbles

Equally delicious are Belgian cookies such as *speculoos* (slightly spicy biscuits), *pain à la Grècque* (a light biscuit with sugar), *pain d'amandes* (butter biscuit with shaved almonds) and *pain d'épices* (a cake with cinnamon and candied fruits). Destrooper is a good brand and is stocked in supermarkets.

TRENDY SHOPPING

Brussels is slowly taking over from Antwerp as Belgium's fashion capital. The Brussels tourist office, on Grand' Place, publishes a useful brochure called *Fashionable Districts* that reveals the obvious fashion districts as well as upcoming places such as St.-Gilles, rue du Bailli and place du Châtelain. In the old St-Boniface quarter you'll find new designers and stores as well as hip bars and restaurants. Most Belgian designers, including Walter Van Beirendonck, Ann Demeulemeester, Dries Van Noten, Dirk Bikkembergs, Veronique Branquinho and Chris Mestdagh, are available at the Stijl (▷ 41), the store that is the grand temple of Belgian fashion. These designers produce accessible avant-garde fashion, while designers such as Olivier Strelli produce more commercial clothes.

Liquid Refreshment

Beer is another good buy, with 700 labels to choose from. Every bar has a beer menu, so you might want to try a few varieties before deciding which to stock up on. Larger super-markets have a good selection of beers, and beer shops can be found in tourist areas in both cities.

Lace, Tapestry and Fashion

Belgium was famous in the Middle Ages for its tapestry and exquisite lace, and there is still plenty of it for sale, although very little is now handmade in Belgium and what you can find is usually very pricey. Belgian fashion design-ers enjoy worldwide success, so take a closer look at their work in Brussels, particularly in and around rue Antoine Dansaert. Local design-ers such as Dries Van Noten, Martin Margiela and Veronique Branquinho create innovative designs based on Belgian traditions.

Art and Comics

Art galleries are all over Brussels—for details obtain a copy of the brochure *Art Brussels* from the tourist office. Many shops specialize in comic books, but none so much as the Tintin shop (▷ 40). Here you can choose from a selection of Tintin books, collectibles, clothes, towels and even wallpaper.

SHOPPING DISTRICTS

The main shopping streets in Bruges are Geldmuntstraat-Noordzandstraat and Steenstraat-Zuidzandstraat. In Brussels, the main shopping street, rue Neuve, has all the international high-street brands and the large shopping mall City 2. The Galeries Royales St.-Hubert (▷ 41) has good traditional shops focusing on design, books, fashion and chocolates. Avenue Louise is Brussels' traditional shopping area, with everything from Chanel to the Belgian designer Olivier Strelli. The fashionable place to shop, however, is the area around rue Antoine Dansaert (▷ 37, St.-Géry), which has the best shoe shops in Brussels and shops of new designers.

Shopping by Theme

Whether you're looking for a department store, a quirky boutique, or something in between, you'll find it all in Brussels and Bruges. On this page shops are listed by theme. For a more detailed write-up, see the individual listings in Brussels and Bruges by Area.

ANTIQUES AND SECONDHAND GOODS

BRUSSELS
Antik Blaes (▷ 40)
Hôtel des Ventes Vanderkindere (▷ 57)
K. Grusenmeyer (▷ 41)
Look 50 (▷ 58)

BRUGES
Yannick de Hondt (▷ 89)

BELGIAN CHOCOLATE

BRUSSELS
A. M. Sweet (▷ 40)
Godiva (▷ 41)
Mary's (▷ 41)
Pierre Marcolini (▷ 41)

BRUGES
Chocolatier Depla Pol (▷ 88)
Servaas van Mullem (▷ 89)
Spegelaere (▷ 89)

BOOKS

BRUSSELS
Anticyclone des Açores (▷ 40)
Filigranes (▷ 41)
FNAC (▷ 41)

BRUGES
Boekhandel Raaklijn (▷ 88)
De Reyghere (▷ 89)
De Striep (▷ 89)

CRAFTS AND GIFTS

BRUSSELS
Au Grand Rasoir (▷ 40)
La Boutique de Tintin (▷ 40)
Christa Reniers (▷ 40)
Plaizier (▷ 41)
Senteurs d'Ailleurs (▷ 58)

BRUGES
'T Apostelientje (▷ 88)
Bazar Bizar (▷ 88)
Brugs Diamanthuis (▷ 88)
Dille & Kamille (▷ 88)
Kantcentrum (Lace Centre) (▷ 89)

FASHION

BRUSSELS
Christophe Coppens (▷ 40)
Church's (▷ 57)
Les Enfants d'Edouard (▷ 57)
Hunting & Collecting (▷ 58)
Martin Margiela (▷ 41)
Natan Couture (▷ 58)
Stijl (▷ 41)

BRUGES
L'Heroïne (▷ 88)
Massimo Dutti (▷ 89)
Olivier Strelli (▷ 89)

FOOD AND DRINK

BRUSSELS
Au Suisse (▷ 40)
Dandoy (▷ 40)
De Coninck (▷ 57)
Marché Place du Châtelain (▷ 58)
Patisserie Wittamer (▷ 41)

BRUGES
The Bottle Shop (▷ 88)
Deldycke (▷ 88)
Diksmuids Boterhuis (▷ 88)
Malesherbes (▷ 89)

OFFBEAT AND UNUSUAL

BRUSSELS
Art Deco 1920–1940 (▷ 57)
Baltazar (▷ 57)
Beer Mania (▷ 57)
Le Dépôt d'Ixelles (▷ 57)
Espace Bizarre (▷ 40)
Serneels (▷ 58)

BRUGES
Hoet Optiek (▷ 89)
The Old Curiosity Shop (▷ 89)
Rombaux (▷ 89)

Brussels and Bruges by Night

The Belgian joke that there's a bar on every corner can't be far from the truth. What's more, licensing laws permit them to stay open as long as they like—often until dawn.

Enjoying a Drink

The bar scene is lively in both cities, as this is what locals do when they go out at night. Even if they go out for dinner or to a show, they still end up having a beer in a bar. The pace of drinking is usually slow but steady, making it easier to keep going all night. In Brussels you can start on the Grand' Place, where the view comes at a price. Nearby there are trendy bars around place St.-Géry and rue du Marché au Charbon, as well as pricier establishments around Le Sablon. Look in Les Marolles or St.-Gilles for distinctively *Bruxellois* cafés, stained dark from decades of tobacco smoke. For jazz clubs and wine bars, try Ixelles.

An Evening Stroll

In Brussels, head for the Grand' Place, beautifully floodlit around at night. In Bruges, the liveliest areas are the Eiermarkt and 't Zand.

Outdoor Living

In summer, Belgians spend long evenings sitting on café terraces chatting. The best in Brussels include Le Roy d'Espagne, La Lunette, Le Falstaff (▷ 45) and the café terraces on the place du Grand Sablon. In Bruges, most people head for cafés on Eiermarkt and 't Zand.

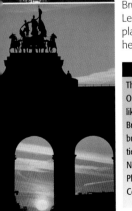

WHAT'S ON

The English-language weekly *The Bulletin* has a "What's On" supplement, or pick up one of the free city guides, like *Agenda* or *RifRaf* (www.rifraf.be) in Brussels, or *Exit* in Bruges. All have entertainment listings in French or Flemish, but it's pretty easy to identify what's going on. In Brussels, tickets to events can be bought from FNAC (in City 2, rue Neuve ☎ 02 275 1111), the tourist office on the Grand' Place or the venue; in Bruges from the tourist office in Concertgebouw, on 't Zand (☎ 050 476 999).

Eating Out

Belgians love to eat and they do it well. Brussels and Bruges have no shortage of excellent restaurants offering Belgian and international fare, prepared with fresh ingredients and served in simple but convivial surroundings. This is true for most eateries, from the simple bistro to the ultimate palace of haute cuisine.

Belgian Dishes

Contrary to popular belief, there is more to Belgian food than *moules frites. Waterzooi* is a little-known national dish, a delicate green stew of fish or chicken with leeks, parsley and cream. Plain but delicious, *stoemp* is potatoes mashed with vegetables, often served with sausages. *Carbonnade flamande* is beef braised in beer with carrots and thyme, and *lapin à la gueuze* is rabbit stewed in gueuze beer with prunes. *Anguilles au vert/paling in het groen* (river eels in green sauce) is another popular dish. A real treat are Belgian waffles, eaten with icing sugar, whipped cream or fruit.

Vegetarian Choices

Belgians like their meat, but options are available for vegetarians. For those who eat it, there is always plenty of fish on the menu. Salads are a popular choice for lunch and vegetarians will find plenty of meat-free dishes in ethnic restaurants, as well as in some specifically vegetarian restaurants. For vegetarian restaurant suggestions in Brussels (▷ 62). In Bruges, try Lotus (▷ 92).

FRITES, FRITES, FRITES

Belgium claims the best fries in the world. The secret of their *frites* is that they are fried twice and thrown into the air to get rid of the extra oil. Every Belgian has a preferred *friture* or *frietkot*, but most agree that Maison Antoine (▷ 62), on place Jourdan in Brussels, and La Barrière St.-Gilles, at chaussée d'Alsemberg in St.-Gilles 3, are the best. In Bruges, have a cone of piping hot *frieten* from the *frietkot* on the Markt.

Restaurants by Cuisine

There are restaurants to suit all tastes and budgets in Brussels and Bruges. On this page they are listed by cuisine. For a more detailed description of each restaurant, see Brussels and Bruges by Area.

BARS AND CAFÉS

BRUSSELS
Brasserie Verschueren (▷ 60)
Café Belga (▷ 60)
Le Cercle des Voyageurs (▷ 44)
Daringman (▷ 45)
Le Falstaff (▷ 45)

BRUGES
'T Brugs Beertje (▷ 91)
Café Vlissinghe (▷ 91)
L'Estaminet (▷ 91)
Est Wijnbar (▷ 91)
Heer Halewijn (▷ 92)
De Republiek (▷ 92)

BELGIAN AND BRASSERIES

BRUSSELS
Au Vieux Bruxelles (▷ 60)
Belga Queen (▷ 44)
Le Clan des Belges (▷ 60)
Le Framboisier Doré (sorbets; ▷ 60)
Maison Antoine (▷ 62)
Le Pain Quotidien (▷ 45)
Taverne du Passage (▷ 46)
De Ultieme Hallucinatie (▷ 46)
L'Ultime Atome (▷ 62)
Vincent (▷ 46)

BRUGES
Breydel de Coninc (▷ 91)
Cafedraal (▷ 91)
Chez Olivier (▷ 91)

Christophe (▷ 91)
Den Dyver (▷ 91)
Jan van Eyck (▷ 92)
Lotus (▷ 92)

BEST DINING

BRUSSELS
La Belle Maraîchère (▷ 44)
Chez Marie (▷ 60)
Comme Chez Soi (▷ 44)
Domaine de Lintillac (▷ 45)
La Manufacture (▷ 45)
La Quincaillerie (▷ 62)
Vismet (▷ 46)
Viva M'Boma (▷ 46)

BRUGES
Den Gouden Harynck (▷ 92)
De Karmeliet (▷ 92)

INTERNATIONAL CUISINE

BRUSSELS
Aux Mille et Une Nuits (Tunisian; ▷ 60)
Bocconi (Italian; ▷ 44)

Bonsoir Clara (Mediterranean; ▷ 44)
Comocomo (tapas; ▷ 44)
Divino (Italian; ▷ 45)
Le Fils de Jules (Basque; ▷ 60)
Gioconda Store Convivio (Italian; ▷ 62)
Le Hasard des Choses (Mediterranean; ▷ 62)
L'Horloge du Sud (West African; ▷ 62)
Kasbah (Moroccan; ▷ 45)
Little Asia (Vietnamese; ▷ 45)
Sahbaz (Turkish; ▷ 46)

BRUGES
De Florentijnen (Italian; ▷ 91)
Rock Fort (Mediterranean; ▷ 92)
Ryad (Moroccan; ▷ 92)
Tanuki (Japanese; ▷ 92)

Top Tips For...

However you'd like to spend your time in Brussels and Bruges, these top suggestions should help you tailor your ideal visit. Each sight or listing has a fuller write-up elsewhere in the book.

A LAZY MORNING

Immerse yourself in the junk market at place du Jeu de Balle in the Marolles district of Brussels (▷ 36) on a Sunday morning.
Linger over a coffee and a delicious pastry at Le Pain Quotidien (▷ 45) in Brussels.
Walk through the park that covers the old city walls around Bruges (▷ 82).

ART NOUVEAU ARCHITECTURE

Head for Victor Horta's own house in Brussels, now the splendid Horta Museum (▷ 52–53).
Rent a bicycle and cycle past Brussels' many art nouveau monuments (▷ 56).
Visit a museum: The Musée des Instruments de Musique (▷ 32) or the Centre Belge de la Bande Dessinée (▷ 24) are both superb examples of Brussels' art nouveau architecture.

Facade of the Musée des Instruments de Musique (above) and the Marolles flea market (top)

SHOPPING SPREES

For Belgian fashion head for Stijl (▷ 41) and other stores in Brussels' rue Antoine Dansaert and the surrounding area.
For designer labels Brussels' avenue Louise is your ticket to paradise.
For antiques visit the weekend antiques market on the Sablon (▷ 34).

ROMANTIC EVENING STROLLS

Take in the Grand' Place, spectacularly lit at night (▷ 26–27).
Walk along the canals in the heart of Bruges (▷ 70).

Take an evening stroll in Bruges' Markt (right)

Don't forget to sample some delicious Belgian chocolates (below)

CHOCOLATES

Visit the high temple of chocolate, Pierre Marcolini's grand and stylish shop (▷ 41) on the Sablon in Brussels.
Learn about the history of chocolate and how the Belgian pralines are made at Bruges' Choco-Story (▷ 71).
Taste the best chocolates, hand-made in small patisseries such as Spegelaere (▷ 89) in Bruges and Mary's (▷ 41) in Brussels.

CULTURE TRAILS

Admire the Flemish Primitives in all their glory at Bruges' Groeninge Museum (▷ 72–73) and Hans Memling Museum (▷ 80–81) or Brussels' Musée d'Art Ancien (▷ 30–31).
Take time to view the facades of each house on the Grand' Place in Brussels (▷ 26–27).
Hitch a ride on one of the canal boats in Bruges (▷ 70) to understand why the city is known as "Venice of the North."

The flower market on Grand' Place (above) and a boat on Bruges' Groenerei (above middle)

BELGIAN CUISINE

Try the exquisite offal dishes at one of Brussels' most acclaimed restaurants, Viva M'Boma (▷ 46).

Watch the waiter prepare a spectacular steak tartare (raw beef) at your table at Vincent (▷ 46).
Enjoy the ultimate Belgian culinary delights at the two-Michelin-star Comme Chez Soi (▷ 44), but reserve well in advance.

The kitchen at Comme Chez Soi (left)

STAYING IN LUXURY

Rocco Forte's Amigo Hotel (▷ 112) hits the right spot—a stylish, luxurious hotel with immaculate service, located right next to Brussels' Grand' Place.
The Warwick Barsey in Brussels (▷ 112) offers stylish yet homey luxury and is close to the shops.
De Orangerie (▷ 112) is one of Bruges' most romantic hotels, in a 15th-century convent next to one of the city's most beautiful canals.

INTIMATE HOTELS

Hotel Montanus (▷ 111) in Bruges is a charming boutique hotel located in a 17th-century mansion.
Le Dixseptième, in a great location in Brussels (▷ 112), offers charming rooms in a beautifully restored 17th-century building.

Enjoy opera at Théatre Royal de la Monnaie (above) or rides at Walibi (below)

OPERA AND DANCE

Witness world-class opera and marvel at the opulent decor at the national opera house of Théâtre Royal de la Monnaie (▷ 37), in Brussels.
Watch and hear local and international dance and music at Bruges' Concertgebouw (▷ 83), the city's 21st-century landmark.

KEEPING THE KIDS HAPPY

Buy kids' fashion by mainly Belgian designers from the kids' store of Stijl (▷ 41), Kat en Muis, at rue Antoine Dansaert 34 in Brussels.
Brave the rides at the theme park Walibi (▷ 106).
Watch the dolphins and enjoy the fairground at the Boudewijn Seapark in Bruges (▷ 102).

Sights	24–37
Walk	38
Shopping	40–41
Entertainment and Nightlife	42–43
Restaurants	44–46

CENTRAL BRUSSELS

Sights	50–55
Bicycle Tour	56
Shopping	57–58
Entertainment and Nightlife	59
Restaurants	60–62

SOUTH BRUSSELS

Sights	66–86
Walk	87
Shopping	88–89
Entertainment and Nightlife	90
Restaurants	91–92

BRUGES

Sights	96–102
Excursions	103–106

FARTHER AFIELD

The Lower Town, around the Grand' Place, is the historical heart of Brussels. The Upper Town, on a steep hill, is home to royalty, state institutions and art museums.

Sights	24–37	Top 25	TOP 25
Walk	38	Centre Belge de la Bande Dessinée ▷ 24	
Shopping	40–41	Hôtel de Ville ▷ 25	
		Grand' Place ▷ 26	
		Manneken-Pis ▷ 28	
Entertainment and Nightlife	42–43	Musée d'Art Moderne ▷ 29	
		Musée d'Art Ancien ▷ 30	
		Musée des Instruments de Musique ▷ 32	
Restaurants	44–46	Place Royale ▷ 33	
		Le Sablon ▷ 34	

DU BD
WERKLIN
Rogier BOULEVARD DU JARDIN BOTANIQUE
City 2
P
Clinique
Saint Jean
Rue de la Blanchisserie
N D du Finistère
Institute et
Fac Saint Louis
BOULEVARD
Botanique /
Kruidtuin
BISCHOFFSHEIM
Musée
du Jouet
Rue de la Sablonnière
Place des
Barricades
Congrès
Kongres
Cité
Administrative
Rue du Nord
Place de
Congrès
Rue du
Gouvernement
Provisoire
Centre Belge
da la Bande
Dessinée
Colonne du
Congrès
Congrès
Kongres
Place de la
Liberté
Rue du Congrès
Rue des
Comédiens
Banque
Nationale
Bank
Cathédrale
des Sts Michel
et Gudule
Rue de l'Enseignement
Cirque
Royale
Rue de la Presse
Place et Parvis
Saint Gudule
Rue des Colonies
Parc /
Park
Rue   de   Louvain
Vlaams
Parlement
GARE CENTRALE
CENTRAAL STATION
Parc
Park
Place de la
Nation
Palais de la
Nation
Rue   de   la   Loi
Hertog
LAAN
R20
REGENT
S G B
Ravenstein
Théâtre
Royal du Parc
Pal des
Congrès
BOZAR
Parc de Bruxelles
Park van Brussel
Mont
des Arts
Musée des Instruments
de Musique
Palais / Paleizen
Musée
d'Art
Moderne
PLACE DES PALAIS
Rue   Ducale
Palais des
Académies
Place
Royale
Musée
d'Art
ncien
Musée BELvue
(BELvue Museum)
Royale /
Koning
Saint
Jacques-sur-
Coudenberg
Palais du Roi
Palais van de
Koning
RUE
DUCALE
Cour des
Comptes
REGENCE
Eglise
Notre-Dame
du Sablon
Rue   de   Namur
Rue Brederodestraat
Place du
Trône
Sablon
e Zavel
Palais
d'Egmont
Porte de Namur
Naamsepoort
Rue de la Pépinière
BOULEVARD
d'Egmont
montuinen
WATERLOOLAAN

0   250 m
0   250 yds

E   F   G

Centre Belge de la Bande Dessinée

Cheerful cartoons at the Centre Belge de la Bande Dessinée (below)

THE BASICS

www.comicscenter.net

🚇 E4

✉ Rue des Sables 20

☎ 02 219 1980

🕐 Tue–Sun 10–6. Closed Christmas Day and New Year's Day

🍴 Restaurant/bar

🚉 Gare Centrale/Centraal Station or de Brouckère

🚋 Tram 4, 32, 55, 56

♿ Good

💷 Moderate

DID YOU KNOW?

● Tintin books have been translated into more than 51 languages.

● The Maison de la Bande Dessinée is at boulevard de l'Impératrice 1 (☎ 02 502 9468, www.jije.org), with the works of Joseph Gillain, known under the pencil name of Jijé, and the young artists he helped to set up.

● Brussels has a Comic Strip Route (6km/4 miles), with the most famous characters painted on facades. A map is available from the tourist office on Grand' Place or at www.brusselsinternational.be.

Captain Haddock: "Land Ho! Land Ho! Thundering typhoons! Land...about time, too!" Tintin: "Why?...Are we out of fuel-oil?" Haddock: "Worse than that!...We're out of whisky!!"—*Hergé's The Adventures of Tintin: The Shooting Star.*

Comic strips and more comic strips Combining comic strips and art nouveau, this is one of Brussels' unusual delights. Although comic strips, or *bds* (*bandes dessinées*), were not invented in Belgium, Belgian artists took the form to new heights. The most famous of them is Hergé (Georges Remi), with his 1929 creations Tintin and Milou (Snowy). The Museum Bookshop stocks thousands of comic strips and collectibles and there is an excellent art nouveau brasserie.

Hands-on entertainment The mezzanine houses an extensive archive, a cinema and an exhibition explaining how *bds* are made. On the upper floor, sections are devoted to each of the great Belgian *bd* creators, with pages to admire as well as hands-on exhibits. The lower floor shows work by Victor Horta (▷ 52–53).

The Magasins Waucquez The collection is housed in the old Waucquez fabric store that opened in 1906. It is a masterpiece of art nouveau, designed by Victor Horta, with a sweeping staircase, glass skylights and plant motifs. The building fell into disrepair in the 1970s, but was beautifully restored in the 1990s to become a museum.

Hôtel de Ville

Had architect Jan van Ruysbroeck foreseen how much his elegant bell tower for the Hôtel de Ville would be admired today, perhaps he would not (as legend has it) have thrown himself off it. The Town Hall itself is a Gothic masterpiece.

A work of art Flanders and Brabant have a wealth of Gothic town halls, but the Brussels Hôtel de Ville is probably the most beautiful of all. It was started in the spring of 1402; the right wing was added in 1444. The octagonal tower, 96m (315ft) high, was added later by architect Jan van Ruysbroeck and bears a gilt statue of the Archangel St. Michael. The top of the tower, 400 steps up, gives the best views over the Grand' Place. Most sculptures adorning the facade of the Town Hall are 19th-century replacements of 14th- and 15th-century originals that are now in the Musée de la Ville de Bruxelles (▷ 37). The court-yard has two 18th-century fountains against the west wall, representing Belgium's most important rivers—the Meuse (to the left) and Scheldt (right).

The Grand Staircase The Grand Staircase carries the busts of all the mayors of Brussels since Belgian independence in 1830. Count Jacques Lalaing painted the murals on the walls in 1893.

The Gothic Hall The splendid 16th-century Council Chamber is decorated with lavish 19th-century tapestries depicting the city's main guilds and crafts. There is a flourish of gilt moldings and the oak floor is inlaid with ebony.

THE BASICS

🚇 E5
✉ Grand' Place
☎ 02 279 0447
🕐 Guided tours only, in English; Apr–Sep Tue, Wed 3.15pm, Sun 10.45am, 12.15pm
🚇 Gare Centrale/Centraal Station or Bourse/Beurse
🚋 Tram 3, 4, 31, 32
♿ Good
💷 Moderate

HIGHLIGHTS

● Grand Staircase
● Bell tower
● Magnificent tapestries

Grand' Place

HIGHLIGHTS

● Hôtel de Ville (▷ 25)
● La Maison du Roi houses the Museé de la Ville de Bruxelles (▷ 37)
● Elegant dome of Roy d'Espagne
● Bronze plaques of Charles Buls and Everard 't Serclaes, left of Hôtel de Ville, to be stroked for good luck
● No. 10 L'Arbre d'Or (Golden Tree) is the Musée des Brasseurs Belges

In the morning, the sun lights up the gilded Gothic, Renaissance and baroque facades of one of the world's most stunning squares. This is the unquestionable heart of Brussels.

Early days By the 11th century, the Grand' Place was already humming as a marketplace, and by the 13th century the first three guildhalls had been built here, for the butchers, bakers and clothmakers. The guilds were trade organizations that regulated working conditions and hours, as well as the trade outside the town. As the guilds became increasingly powerful, they even took part in a number of wars, and commanded ever higher membership fees. The guilds' might is never more palpable than when you stand in the Grand' Place. Destroyed by a

Clockwise from left: a regal statue crowns the Maison du Roi; horses and flagbearers take part in the vivid *Ommegang* pageant, as people look on; a statue tops Le Roy d'Espagne building; a group of life-size Meyboom Puppets pose for a photograph

French bombardment in 1695 (except for the Hôtel de Ville, ▷ 25), the square was entirely rebuilt by the guilds in less than five years.

The guildhalls Each one in the Grand' Place is distinguished by statues and ornate carvings. Look for No. 5 La Louve (the She-Wolf), representing the archers' guild; No. 7 Le Renard (Fox), the haberdashers' guild; No. 9 Le Cygne (Swan), the butchers' guild, where Karl Marx and Friedrich Engels wrote *The Communist Manifesto* in 1848; Nos. 24–25 La Chaloupe d'Or (Golden Galleon), the tailors' guild; and No. 26–27 Le Pigeon, representing the painters' guild, where novelist Victor Hugo stayed in 1852. Of particular interest are Nos. 29–33, the Maison du Roi, called the Broodhuis in Flemish; it belonged not to a king but to the bakers' guild.

THE BASICS

✚ E5
🍴 Restaurants on square
🚇 Gare Centrale/Centraal Station or Bourse/Beurs
🚊 Tram 3, 4, 31, 32
♿ Good
💷 Free
❓ Mid-Dec Christmas fair with Christmas tree, shopping, food and concerts

Manneken-Pis

Left to right: Europe Day celebrations; Mannekin uncovered; posing for that must-have photo

THE BASICS

➕ D5

✉ Corner of rue de l'Etuve and rue du Chêne

🚈 Gare Centrale/Centraal Station or Bourse/Beurs

🚌 48, 95; tram 3, 4, 31, 32

♿ Free

❓ For the dates when Manneken-Pis is dressed up, see the sign at the statue

DID YOU KNOW?

● In 1985, feminists demanded a female version of Manneken-Pis and commissioned Jeanneke Pis (✉ Impasse de la Fidelité, off rue des Bouchers).

● Every 13 September Manneken-Pis wears the uniform of a sergeant in the Regiment of Welsh Guards to celebrate the liberation of Brussels in 1944.

If it were not for the bus-loads of tourists who gather in front of this little fellow to have their picture taken, it would be easy to walk past him—a strange mascot for a city.

Cheeky cherub Manneken-Pis, meaning "pissing little boy," is one of Brussels' more amusing symbols. The bronze statuette, less than 60cm (2ft) high, was created by Jerôme Duquesnoy the Elder in 1619. Known then as "Petit Julien," it has since become a legend. One story claims that the Julien on whom the statue was modeled was the son of Duke Gottfried of Lorraine; another alleges that the statue memorializes a boy who urinated on a bomb fuse to save the Town Hall from destruction.

Often vandalized The statue was kidnapped by the English in 1745, as a way of getting at the people of Brussels; two years later the French took him away. In 1817 he was stolen by a French convict and was in pieces when he was recovered. The fragments were used to make the mold for the present statue. Even now he remains a temptation: He has been removed several times by drunk or angry students.

An extravagant wardrobe The French king Louis XV gave him a richly embroidered robe and the cross of Louis XIV as reparation for the bad actions of his soldiers in 1747. Now, Manneken-Pis has some 800 costumes, which you can see in the Musée de la Ville de Bruxelles (▷ 37), a few streets away on the Grand' Place.

TOP 25

Musée d'Art Moderne

This museum puts modern Belgian artists in their context, and many of them shine, even among the great European stars. The venue also stages important temporary exhibitions.

20th-century Belgians Belgian artists are sometimes overlooked in preference for their other European contemporaries, so perhaps there is something symbolic in the fact that the Modern Art Museum (which together with the Musée d'Art Ancien comprise the Musées Royaux des Beaux-Arts de Belgique) is buried in a subterranean building. But a visit reveals outstanding works.

Fauvists and surrealists In the early 20th century, local artists were interested by fauvism, best represented by the works of Rik Wouters, Auguste Oleffe and Léon Spilliaert, and surrealism, which grew out of the post-World War I chaos. Belgians René Magritte and Paul Delvaux are two stars of surrealism, and the museum collection includes one of Magritte's most famous paintings *The Dominion of Light*. Among the foreign artists represented here are Max Ernst, Francis Picabia, James Ensor and Oskar Kokoschka.

Other movements The lower levels show Belgian futurism, abstract art, pop art, new realism and minimal art. Particularly important here is the work of Marcel Broodthaers. A collection of works by Henri Matisse, Raoul Dufy, Picasso, Giorgio de Chirico, Marc Chagall and Dalí helps to put the Belgian artists in a wider context.

THE BASICS

www.fine-arts-museum.be
🔠 E6
✉ Rue de la Régence
☎ 02 508 3211
🕐 Tue–Sun 10–5
🍽 Cafeteria-restaurant
🚇 Gare Centrale/Centraal Station or Trône/Troon
🚌 27, 38, 60, 71, 95, 96; tram 92, 93
♿ Very good
💰 Moderate (free 1st Wed of month from 1pm)
❓ Regular temporary exhibitions as well as readings and music (see Friends of the Museum, www.becomeafriend.be ☎ 02 511 4116)

HIGHLIGHTS

● *Dominion of Light* and others, René Magritte
● *The Flautist* and *The Woman with the Yellow Necklace*, Rik Wouters
● *Skeletons Fighting Over a Smoked Herring*, James Ensor, 1891
● *The Public Voice* and *Pygmalion*, Paul Delvaux

CENTRAL BRUSSELS TOP 25

Musée d'Art Ancien

HIGHLIGHTS

● *Landscape with the Fall of Icarus* and *The Census at Bethlehem*, Brueghel
● *The Ascent to Calvary* and *The Martyrdom of St. Lievin*, Rubens
● *Portrait of Anthony of Burgundy*, Dirk Bouts
● *The Justice of the Emperor Otto*, Dirk Bouts
● *The Scandalized Masks*, James Ensor
● *The Temptation of St. Anthony*, School of Hieronymus Bosch
● Sculpture garden next to the museum

The Museum of Old Art highlights how rich a period the 14th to 17th centuries were for Belgian art, with works by Pieter Brueghel the Elder, Rubens, the Flemish Primitives, and other European masters like Tintoretto and Rembrandt.

Museum history The Old Art Museum and the nearby Museum of Modern Art (▷ 29) were founded by Napoleon in 1801 as the Museum of Brussels. The Old Art Museum is in a building constructed in 1874–80 by Leopold II's colonial architect, Alphonse Balat. It saw complete modernization in the 1980s and is now connected to the Museum of Modern Art by an underground passage.

Artistic riches The tour of the museum starts with a collection of impressive works by the

Flemish Primitives. They are well represented here with works by Rogier van der Weyden, Dirk Bouts, Hieronymus Bosch, Gerard David and particularly Hans Memling. The museum's collection of the works of the Brueghels is world-class, second only to that in Vienna's Kunst-Historisches Museum. Later artists include Jacob Jordaens.

Sculpture The central Forum, on the first floor, is home to a collection of 19th-century sculptures, including works by Jan van Kessel and Rodin, while the rooms off it contain masterpieces of the Romantic and Classical movements, including paintings by Delacroix.

Sculpture garden The sculpture collection in the garden beside the museum is less well known, but is excellent and well-arranged.

THE BASICS

www.fine-arts-museum.be
✚ E6
✉ Rue de la Régence 3
☎ 02 508 3211
🕐 Tue–Sun 10–5
🍴 Cafeteria-restaurant
🚇 Gare Centrale/Centraal Station or Trône/Troon
🚌 27, 34, 38, 60, 71, 95, 96; tram 92, 93
♿ Good
💰 Moderate (free 1st Wed of month from 1pm)
❓ Regular exhibitions, music and readings (see Friends of the Museum, www.becomeafriend.be, tel: 02 511 4116)

Musée des Instruments de Musique

The museum's distinctive art nouveau facade (left); pianos on display (below)

THE BASICS

www.mim.fgov.be

➕ E6

✉ Rue Montagne de la Cour 2

☎ 02 545 0130

🕐 Tue–Fri 9.30–5, Sat, Sun 10–5

🍴 Bar and restaurant (on top floor, with summer terrace)

🚇 Gare Centrale/Centraal Station or Parc/Park

🚋 Tram 92, 93

♿ Good

💶 Expensive; free 1st Wed of the month after 1pm

❓ Walking tours every Fri, 10.30–12, about the history of a particular instrument. Workshops in music, dance, and the making of instruments

DID YOU KNOW?

● Giacomo Puccini died in 1924 in a hospital near the place du Trône, in Brussels.

● Adolphe Sax, the Belgian musician who invented the saxophone in 1846, studied at the Royal Music Conservatoire in Brussels, where Clara Schumann, Hector Berlioz, Niccolò Paganini, Richard Wagner and many others appeared.

The Museum of Musical Instruments is a pleasure to visit, both for its amazing collection and for the art nouveau architecture of its "Old England" building.

The collection When in 1877 King Leopold II received a large number of Hindu instruments from Rajah Sourindro Mohun Tagore, and at the same time the musicologist Jean-François Fétis donated his collection to the State, it was decided to create a Museum of Musical Instruments. Since then the museum has acquired instruments from across the centuries and from all over the world. Today, with more than 7,000 instruments, one quarter of which are on display, it is one of the most important museums of its kind in the world. The bulk of the collection is European, from the Renaissance onward. Every instrument is beautifully displayed, and some are astonishing, like the glass harmonica designed by the American inventor and statesman Benjamin Franklin (1706–90), for which both Beethoven and Mozart wrote music, or the 18th-century *pochettes*, tiny violins that violin teachers could carry in their pockets. Using a headset, you can listen to music played by the instrument at which you are looking.

Old England Building The Old England Department Store, in which the museum is housed, was designed in 1899 by Paul Saintenoy. Inspired by the British Arts and Crafts movement, he decided upon a grand art nouveau style building with cast-iron pillars, swirling wrought iron, painted floral decoration and lots of natural light.

The Royal Palace's Throne Room (below); statue of Godefroid de Bouillon (right)

Place Royale

This elegant neoclassical square is anchored by some powerful institutions: the Royal Palace, the Belgian Parliament and the Law Courts.

Symmetrical square Place Royale was built in 1774–80, an enclosed rectangle made up of eight palaces joined by porticoes. At the heart stands the statue of Godefroid de Bouillon, who led the first crusade in the 11th century. Rue de la Régence links the square with the imposing Law Courts, and at the other end is the Parc de Bruxelles, designed by Guimard in c.1775 and once the royal hunting grounds. On the east side is the Église St.-Jacques-sur-Coudenberg.

Museums The palace of Charles de Lorraine (1766) is a lovely neoclassical building just off the square, under which sits the Museum of Modern Art (▷ 29). You can visit the north wing of the palace to see objects that reveal Charles's interest in the Enlightenment. The Hôtel Bellevue, near the Palais Royal, now houses the fascinating Musée BELvue (▷ 36), focusing on Belgian history, which also gives access to the remains of the 11th-century Coudenberg Palace. Victor Horta's Palais des Beaux Arts (1928) is now a lively arts space (BOZAR, ▷ 35) with a Film Museum next door.

Palais Royal On nearby place des Palais is the Palais Royal, the King's official residence, although in the last decades the royals have lived in their Laeken palace (▷ 102). The Palais de la Nation, on rue de la Loi, is now the Belgian Parliament.

THE BASICS

✚ E6

🚇 Trône/Gare Centrale/Centraal Station

🚋 Tram 92, 94

Église St.-Jacques-sur-Coudenberg

🕐 Mon 12–2, Tue–Fri 12–5.45, Sat 1–5.45, Sun 8.30–7

♿ None 🎫 Free

Palais Royal

🕐 22 Jul–7 Sep, Tue–Sun 10.30–4.30

♿ Good 🎫 Free

HIGHLIGHTS

● Old and Modern Art Museums (▷ 29–31)
● Palace of Charles de Lorraine
● A stroll in the Parc de Bruxelles, with its tree-lined avenue and fountain

DID YOU KNOW?

● The Brussels Card (24 hrs €24, 48 hrs €36, 72 hrs €43) offers free entry to over 30 museums, free use of public transport and exclusive offers at shops, exhibitions, restaurants and various attractions.

CENTRAL BRUSSELS TOP 25

Le Sablon

Browsing the weekend antiques market at Le Sablon

THE BASICS

🞤 E6
☎ Church: 02 511 5741
🕐 Church: Mon–Fri 9–6.30, Sat, Sun 9–7
🍴 Restaurants, cafés
🚌 20, 21; tram 92, 93
♿ Good
❓ Antiques market Sat 9–5, Sun 9–2

HIGHLIGHTS

● Église Notre Dame du Sablon
● Statues on place du Petit Sablon
● Antiques market and shops
● Garden behind Palais d'Egmont
● Patisserie Wittamer (▷ 41)
● Pierre Marcolini chocolates (▷ 41)

The Sablon district, with its Grand and Petit Sablon squares, is the focus of the antiques trade. It is also perfect for strolling, and its terraces are lovely places to sit and watch the world go by.

Place du Grand Sablon Many of Brussels' 17th-century aristocracy and bourgeoisie lived in this elegant square, which is now popular with antiques traders. The square has many specialist food shops, including Patisserie Wittamer (▷ 41), selling wonderful cakes, and Pierre Marcolini (▷ 41), with amazing chocolates.

Place du Petit Sablon Mayor Charles Buls commissioned this square in 1890. The statue of the Counts of Egmont and Horne, who were beheaded by the Duke of Alba during the wars of religion, was moved here from the Grand' Place and is surrounded by statues of 16th-century scholars and humanists. Behind the garden, the 16th-century Palais d'Egmont, rebuilt in the early 20th century after a fire, is used for receptions by the Ministry of Foreign Affairs.

Église Notre Dame du Sablon The 15th-century church of Notre Dame du Sablon is a fine example of flamboyant Gothic architecture, built over an earlier chapel with a miraculous statue of the Virgin Mary. A hemp weaver from Antwerp heard celestial voices telling her to steal the Madonna statue at the church where she worshiped and take it to Brussels. The choir and stained-glass windows are particularly beautiful.

BOURSE

The Belgian Stock Exchange is in an elegant 1873 building with a frieze by Albert-Ernest Carrier-Belleuse and sculptures by Auguste Rodin. Under the Bourse is the archaeological site of Bruxella 1238—the ruins of a 13th-century Franciscan convent. You can visit this site on the first Wednesday of every month at 11.15am and 3pm.

➕ D5 ✉ Rue Henri Maus 2 ☎ 02 509 1211 🕐 Mon–Fri for groups by prior arrangement 🚇 De Brouckère 🚊 Tram 3, 4, 31, 32 ♿ Few 💶 Inexpensive

BOZAR

www.bozar.be

BOZAR, formally the Palais des Beaux Arts, was designed by Victor Horta in 1928. He left the flamboyant art nouveau style of his earlier buildings behind and opted for a sterner Modernist construction. This is a lively venue for concerts and exhibitions of modern and contemporary art. It also houses the Musée du Cinema.

➕ E5–6 ✉ Rue Ravenstein 23 ☎ 02 507 8200 🚇 Parc/Park ♿ Good 💶 Varies

CATHÉDRALE DES STS. MICHEL ET GUDULE

www.cathedralestmichel.be

With its intriguing mixture of styles and influences, the cathedral of Sts. Michael and Gudule expresses Brussels' ability to compromise and is a fitting venue for state occasions. The earlier Romano-Gothic elements, particularly the ambulatory and choir, fit happily with those from the Late Gothic period, which are in the nave and on the west facade. Restoration work since 1983 has exposed elements of an earlier church (founded 1047), on which the cathedral was built.

➕ E5 ✉ Parvis St.-Gudule ☎ 02 217 8345 🕐 Mon–Fri 7–6 (5 in winter), Sat 8.30–3.30, Sun 2–6 (5 in winter) 🚇 Gare Centrale/Centraal Station ♿ Few 💶 Inexpensive

LA CENTRALE ÉLECTRIQUE/ DE ELEKTRICITEITSCENTRALE

www.centrale-art.be

Brussels' first ever power plant, built in 1903, now houses the European Centre for Contemporary Art. The

A 16th-century stained-glass window and the striking facade of the Cathédrale St.-Michel et Ste.-Gudule

large space hosts avant-garde art and organizes workshops for children.

🕀 D4 🖂 Place Ste.-Catherine 44 ☎ 02 279 6452 🕔 Tue–Sun 10.30–6, Thu 11–8 🚇 Ste.-Catherine/St.-Katelijne/Bourse 💵 Moderate

ÉGLISE ST.-NICOLAS

The oldest church in Brussels was founded in the 11th century, but most of the interior dates from the 18th. The curved building once followed the line of the River Senne, and a cannonball in the wall recalls the city's bombardment of 1695.

🕀 E5 🖂 Rue au Beurre 1 ☎ 02 513 8022 🕔 Mon–Fri 8–6.30, Sat 9–6, Sun 9–7.30 🚇 Bourse/Beurs 🚊 Tram 4, 32, 55, 56 💵 Free

LES MAROLLES

Dwarfed by the Palais de Justice and hemmed in by the elegant Sablon quarter, the Marolles is a reminder of working-class Brussels, with its narrow cobbled streets and junk shops. It stretches roughly from the Porte de Hal to the Église Notre-Dame-de-la-Chapelle; rue Blaes and rue Haute are its main thoroughfares. Around place du Jeu de Balle are traditional cafés and junk shops. The flea market held here has unusual items at bargain prices, especially on Sunday mornings. A fashionable crowd is slowly moving into the Marolles, and in recent years several art galleries, trendy cafés and nightclubs have opened their doors.

🕀 D7 🖂 Around place du Jeu de Balle 🚌 27, 95; tram 92, 93 🚶 Few ❓ Flea market daily 7–2

MUSÉE BELVUE

www.belvue.be

This interesting museum reveals the history of Belgium since independence in 1830. It is housed in the Hôtel Bellevue, built in the late 18th century on the ruins of the 11th-century castle of the Dukes of Brabant, later Emperor Charles V's Coudenberg Palace. The museum gives access to the archaeological site of these impressive ruins.

🕀 E–F6 🖂 Place des Palais 7 ☎ 070 220492 🕔 Jun–Sep Tue–Sun 9.30–5; Oct–May Tue–Sun 10–5 🚇 Parc/Park 🚶 Good 💵 Moderate

You'll find no shortage of interesting and unusual items in the flea market at Les Marolles

MUSÉE DE LA VILLE DE BRUXELLES

www.museedelavilledebruxelles.be

This 19th-century building, a careful reconstruction of the original Maison du Roi, is devoted to Brussels' history, and displays paintings, tapestries, maps and manuscripts, as well as the wardrobe of Manneken-Pis (▷ 28). 🔓 E5 ✉ Grand' Place ☎ 02 279 4350 🕐 Tue–Sun 10–5 🚇 Bourse/Beurs, Gare Centrale/Centraal Station ♿ Few 👆 Inexpensive

PALAIS DE JUSTICE

The Palais de Justice was one of Leopold II's pet projects, designed by Joseph Poelaert in grand eclectic style. The interior is as overwhelming as the views over Brussels from the terrace. It still contains the main law courts. 🔓 D–E7 ✉ Place Poelaert ☎ 02 508 6410 🕐 Mon–Fri 9–3. Closed holidays 🚇 Louise/Louiza 🚋 Tram 92, 93 ♿ Very good 👆 Free

ST.-GÉRY AND STE.-CATHERINE

Brussels was founded on the place St.-Géry in 979, when Charles, Duke of Lorraine, built a castle here. Now the square is a happening place, with many bars. Rue Antoine Dansaert has stylish shops and rue des Chartreuses and chaussée de Flandres have great bars and restaurants. For good fish restaurants, try the Marché aux Poissons (Fish Market) off place Ste.-Catherine. 🔓 D4–5 ✉ Around the rue Antoine Dansaert and place St-Géry 🚇 Bourse/Beurs, Ste.-Catherine/St.-Katelijne ♿ Good

THÉÂTRE ROYAL DE LA MONNAIE

www.lamonnaie.be

This 1697 hall was enlarged in 1819 by Napoleon to become one of the most beautiful in the world. It was here the Belgian Revolution began in August 1830. In 1985 the hall was again enlarged, with a ceiling by Sam Francis and tiling by Sol Lewitt. The opera performances are outstanding. 🔓 E4–5 ✉ Place de la Monnaie ☎ 02 229 1200 🚇 De Brouckère ♿ Very good ❓ Tours available

Relaxing in a bar in St-Géry

From Manneken-Pis to Jeanneke-Pis

This walk explores the historical heart of Brussels, with the Grand' Place and the now-trendy area of St.-Géry, where the city was born.

DISTANCE: 1.5km (1 mile) **ALLOW:** 1–2 hours

START

GRAND' PLACE ▷ 26–27
🚇 E5 🚊 Gare Centrale or Bourse

❶ Leave the Grand' Place (▷ 26; pictured right) via rue Charles Buls. Walk along rue de l'Etuve, leading to Manneken-Pis (▷ 28).

❷ Turn right onto rue Grands-Carmes to rue du Marché au Charbon. Walk past Église Notre-Dame du Bon-Secours to boulevard Anspach.

❸ Turn right onto the boulevard and then left onto rue des Riches Claires, with its 17th-century church. Turn right onto rue de la Grande Île.

❹ Immediately left, a passageway leads to the back of the church and the original site of the River Senne. Return to place St.-Géry.

END

RUE DES BOUCHERS
🚇 E5 🚊 Gare Centrale or Bourse

❽ Take a right onto rue des Fripiers and left onto rue Grétry, which becomes rue des Bouchers, where Jeanneke-Pis is signposted.

❼ This leads to place Ste.-Catherine, built on the basin of Brussels' old port. Walk past the Tour Noire, part of the first city wall, back to boulevard Anspach, and cross over onto rue de l'Évêque to place de la Monnaie, with the Théâtre Royal de la Monnaie.

❻ Walk along rue du Pont de la Carpe and then left onto rue Antoine Dansaert, where there are restaurants and trendy clothes shops. Take a right onto rue du Vieux Marché aux Grains.

❺ A plaque on Halles St.-Géry shows the site of Brussels' origins.

Shopping

A. M. SWEET
Tea salon and shop with
beautiful chocolates,
crystallized flowers, *pain
d'épices* and coffees.
✛ D5 ✉ Rue des Chartreux
4 ☎ 02 513 5131 ◷ Tue
12–6.30, Wed–Sat 9.30–6.30
◉ Bourse/Beurs

ANTICYCLONE
DES AÇORES
www.anticyclonedesacores.be
A great travel bookshop
with travel guides, maps,
globes and travel litera-
ture in several languages.
✛ D4 ✉ Rue Fossé aux
Loups 34 ☎ 02 217 5246
◷ Mon–Sat 10.30–6.30
◉ De Brouckère

ANTIK BLAES
Two floors of funky,
European home and
shop furniture (mostly
1940s–1980s), and a
few intriguing curiosities.
✛ D6 ✉ Rue Blaes 51–53
☎ 02 512 1299 ◷ Daily
10–6 ▣ 27, 48

AU GRAND RASOIR
(MAISON JAMART)
www.coutellerie-jamart.be
A beautiful knife shop,
supplier to the royal
family, with an incredible
selection. Repairs,
sharpening, resilvering.
✛ E5 ✉ Rue de l'Hôpital 7
☎ 02 512 4962 ◷ Mon–Sat
9.30–6.30 ◉ Gare Centrale/
Centraal Station ▣ 34, 48, 95

AU SUISSE
www.ausuisse.be
The traditional deli to buy
smoked fish, cheeses,
charcuterie (cold cuts)

and other delicacies. The
sandwich bar next door
of the same name is also
a Brussels institution and
offers snacks from tasty
sandwiches to spaghetti
Bolognese.
✛ D5 ✉ Boulevard Anspach
73–75 ☎ 02 512 9589
◷ Mon–Fri 17.30–6, Sat 10–7
◉ Bourse/Beurs ▣ Tram 3,
4, 31, 32

LA BOUTIQUE
DE TINTIN
www.tintinboutique.com
Tintin fans come here for
everything from pyjamas,
socks, cups, stationery,
postcards and diaries to
life-size statues of Tintin
and his friend Abdullah
and, of course, the books.
✛ D5 ✉ Rue de la Colline
13 ☎ 02 514 5152
◷ Mon–Sat 10–6, Sun 11–5
◉ Gare Centrale/Centraal
Station

CHRISTA RENIERS
www.christareniers.com
Beautiful contemporary
silver and gold jewelry
with a touch of Zen and
no shortage of wit.
Reniers' silver cufflinks
and keyrings are fun, and
the bracelets, rings and
earrings have an elegance
of their own.

✛ E6 ✉ Rue Lebeau 61
☎ 02 514 9154 ◷ Tue–Sat
12.30–6.30, Sun 1–5 ▣ 27,
48, 95; tram 92, 93

CHRISTOPHE
COPPENS
Renowned Belgian hat
maker, who uses all
sorts of materials, from
traditional and classic to
outrageous and wacky.
Most of his designs are
for women but there are
also some for men.
✛ D4 ✉ 2 rue Léon Lepage
☎ 02 538 0813 ◷ Tue–Sat
11–6 ◉ Ste.-Catherine/St.-
Katelijne

DANDOY
www.maisondandoy.com
This bakery, founded
in 1829, sells Brussels
cookies such as *pain à
la Grecque, speculoos*
and *couque de Dinant*
in all sizes and shapes,
as well as Belgium's best
marzipan. Once you are
inside, this place is hard
to resist!
✛ E5 ✉ Rue au Beurre 31
(other branches at rue Charles
Buls 14 and place St.-Job 22)
☎ 02 540 2702 ◷ Mon–Sat
9–7, Sun 10.30–7 ◉ Bourse/
Beurs ▣ Tram 4, 32, 55, 56

ESPACE BIZARRE
www.espacebizzare.com
Large store selling everything for modern living,
from Japanese beds and
Scandinavian furniture to
candles and tableware.
✛ D5 ✉ Rue des Chartreux
19b ☎ 02 514 5256
◷ Mon–Sat 11–7 ◉ Bourse/
Beurs

FILIGRANES
www.filigranes.be
Filigranes—the name means watermarks—stocks mainly French books, but there is a good English-language selection in the basement. They also sell DVDs, CDs, newspapers and magazines, and there is coffee, snacks and even wine available.
➕ F6 ✉ Avenue des Arts 39–42 ☎ 02 511 9015 🕐 Mon–Fri 8–8, Sat 10–7.30, Sun 10–7 🚇 Troon/Trône

FNAC
www.fnac.be
Brussel's largest bookshop, with titles in French, Dutch, English, German, Italian and Spanish, and a good music department.
➕ E4 ✉ City 2, rue Neuve ☎ 02 275 1111 🕐 Mon–Thu, Sat 10–7, Fri 10–8 🚇 Rogier, De Brouckère 🚊 Tram 3, 4, 31, 32

GODIVA
www.godiva.be
The most famous chocolatier of all, with shops around the world.
➕ E5 ✉ Grand' Place 22 ☎ 02 511 2537 🕐 Mon–Sat 9am–11pm, Sun 10am–11pm 🚇 Gare Centrale/ Centraal Station

K. GRUSENMEYER
www.grusenmeyer.be
Wonderful antiques shop specializing in tribal and oriental sculpture and objets d'art, and exquisite 18th- and 19th-century Chinese furniture.

➕ E6 ✉ Rue Lebeau 14 ☎ 02 514 0337 🕐 Mon–Sat 12–6 🚇 Porte de Namur 🚊 Tram 92, 93

MARTIN MARGIELA
www.maisonmartinmargiela.com
Flagship store of the cult Belgian designer.
➕ D4 ✉ Rue de Flandre 114 ☎ 02 223 7520 🕐 Mon–Sat 11–7 🚇 Bourse/Beurs, Ste.-Catherine/Ste.-Katelijne

MARY'S
www.mary.be
This shop specializes in homemade pralines and *marrons glacés,* using the finest ingredients.
➕ F4 ✉ Rue Royale 73 ☎ 02 217 4500 🕐 Mon–Sat 10–6 🚇 Botanique/ Kruidtuin 🚊 Tram 92, 93

PATISSERIE WITTAMER
www.wittamer.com
This wonderful but expensive patisserie sells Brussels' best sorbets, excellent chocolates and cakes that taste fab.
➕ E6 ✉ Place du Grand Sablon 6 and 12–13 ☎ 02

GALERIES ROYALES ST.-HUBERT
This elegant covered arcade has new and traditional stores. It was built in 1846–47, when this type of shopping mall was a first in Europe.
✉ Rue du Marché-aux-Herbes 🚇 Gare Centrale/ Centraal Station ♿ Good

512 3742 🕐 Mon 9–6, Tue–Sat 7–7, Sun 7–6 🚊 Tram 92, 93

PIERRE MARCOLINI
www.marcolini.be
Marcolini is winner of the Chocolatier of the World award, and his chocolate creations are some of the best, and most expensive, in Belgium. (Shops also at 75 avenue Louise and 1302 chaussée de Waterloo.)
➕ E6 ✉ Rue des Minimes 1 ☎ 02 514 1206 🕐 Sun–Thu 10–7, Fri–Sat 10–8 🚊 48, 95; tram 92, 93

PLAIZIER
www.avecplaizier.be
A beautiful shop with an excellent selection of photographic postcards, posters, books and other visually pleasing objects.
➕ E5 ✉ Rue des Éperonniers 50 ☎ 02 513 9929 🕐 Mon–Sat 11–6 (Dec daily 7–7) 🚇 Gare Centrale/Centraal Station

STIJL
www.stijl.be
In her temple of Belgian fashion Sonja Noël stocks established designers like Dries Van Noten and Ann Demeulemeester, and promotes new designers. Down the road at No. 34 is Kat en Muis, her shop for kids.
➕ D4 ✉ Rue Antoine Dansaert 74 ☎ 02 512 0313 🕐 Mon–Sat 10.30–6.30 🚇 Bourse/ Beurs, Ste.-Catherine/St.-Katelijne 🚊 Tram 3, 4, 31, 32

Entertainment and Nightlife

ACTORS STUDIO
www.actorsstudio.cinenews.be
Two-screen repertory cinema showing five films a day, mainly "B" movies and good films from non-European countries.
🔛 E5 ✉ Petite rue des Bouchers 16 ☎ 02 512 1696
🚇 De Brouckère

A LA MORT SUBITE
www.alamortsubite.com
This traditional bar was one of singer Jacques Brel's preferred watering holes. It even has its own brew, called Mort Subite (Sudden Death) because of its higher alcohol content.
🔛 E5 ✉ Rue Montagne aux Herbes Potagères 7 ☎ 02 513 1318 🕐 Mon–Sat 11am–1am, Sun 12–12 🚇 Gare Centrale/Centraal station

ANCIENNE BELGIQUE
www.abconcerts.be
The famous AB has been everything from 15th-century merchants' hall and bank vault to 20th-century music hall and is now one of Brussels' best pop and rock venues.
🔛 D5 ✉ Boulevard Anspach 110 ☎ 02 548 2484
🚇 Bourse/Beurs

L'ARCHIDUC
www.archiduc.net
Funky, smoky art deco lounge designed like a cruise ship. It plays jazz or 1930s music.
🔛 D5 ✉ Rue Antoine Dansaert 6 ☎ 02 512 0652 🕐 Daily 4pm–6am
🚇 Bourse/Beurs

ARENBERG NOMADIC CINEMAS
www.arenberg.be
The Arenberg is a long-established film institution that stages European, Asian and Middle Eastern films in different venues throughout Brussels. Check the website for upcoming programs and for venues around Brussels.
🔛 E4 ✉ Rue Leopold 1
☎ 02 511 6515

BEURSSCHOUWBURG
www.beursschouwburg.be
The 19th-century theater of the Stock Exchange is now a venue for rock concerts, jazz, North African raï and avant-garde Belgian plays.
🔛 D5 ✉ Rue Auguste Orts 20–28 ☎ 02 550 0350
🚇 Bourse/Beurs 🚋 Tram 3, 4, 33

LE BOTANIQUE
www.botanique.be
The botanical gardens are now a cultural complex and music venue for the French-speaking community. See rock concerts in the Orangerie and world music events like the

> **TICKETS**
> Tickets for most big events in Brussels can be booked (at a small charge) through the tourist office on the Grand' Place (☎ 02 513 8940; www.visitbrussels.be) or FNAC in City 2, rue Neuve (☎ 02 275 1111).

Festival de la Chanson in September.
🔛 F4 ✉ Rue Royale 236 ☎ 02 218 3732
🚇 Botanique/Botaniek
🚌 4, 61; tram 92, 93

CAFÉ CENTRAL
www.lecafecentral.com
Small but great venue, with a dance floor in the back and a cinema. Concerts twice a month (usually Thursday 10pm).
🔛 D5 ✉ Rue de Borgval 14
🚇 Bourse/Beurs

CINEMATEK FILMMUSEUM
www.cinematek.be
Besides the permanent exhibition, five films are shown daily. Two are silent films accompanied by piano music. This is the place to see the old cinema classics, as well as more recent movies and little-known jewels from around the world.
🔛 E5–6 ✉ Rue Baron Horta 9 ☎ 02 551 1900 🕐 Daily 5.30–10.30 🚇 Gare Centrale/Centraal Station 🚋 Tram 92, 93

CONSERVATOIRE ROYAL DE MUSIQUE
www.conservatoire.be
Another perfect venue for chamber orchestras.
🔛 E6 ✉ Rue de la Régence 30 ☎ 02 511 0427
🚇 Louise/Louiza

LE FUSE
www.fuse.be
Popular Saturday night venue in a converted cinema, Le Fuse is one

of Belgium's top techno music dance clubs where things hot up from the early hours.

⊞ D7 ⊠ Rue Blaesstraat 208 ☎ 02 511 9789 🕐 Sat–Sun 11pm–7am 🚇 Porte de Hal/ Hallepoort 🚋 3, 4, 51

HALLES DE SCHAERBEEK

www.halles.be
This superb 19th-century covered market is now a major cultural venue for the French-speaking community, with regular music, dance and drama.

⊞ G3 ⊠ Rue Royal Ste.-Marie 22b ☎ 02 218 2107 🚇 Botanique/Botaniek

KAAITHEATER

www.kaaitheater.be
A jewel of 1930s architecture, this former cinema houses the Flemish Theater Institute. There are performances by influential Belgian dancers. The inhouse Kaaicafé opens before and after performances.

⊞ D3 ⊠ Square Sainctelette 20 ☎ 02 201 5959 🚇 Yser/ Ilzer

MIRANO CONTINENTAL

www.mirano.be
Fashionable crowds of thirtysomethings frequent this former cinema, where house music is king. Dress up or they might not let you in.

⊞ G4 ⊠ Chaussée de Louvain 38 ☎ 02 227 3942 🕐 Fri, Sat 10pm–6am 🚇 Madou

MUSIC VILLAGE

www.themusicvillage.com
Lively jazz café with concerts, from the traditional to the most experimental, as well as world music such as flamenco.

⊞ D5 ⊠ Steenstraat 50 ☎ 02 513 5052 🕐 Dinner from 7pm, concerts from 7pm 🚇 De Brouckère, Bourse/ Beurs

PALAIS DES BEAUX ARTS (BOZAR)

www.bozar.be
This art nouveau complex is Brussels' most prestigious concert venue. Its two halls, with perfect acoustics, are home to the Philharmonic Society and the Orchestre National de Belgique. Most of the city's big concerts take place here. The complex boasts a splendid organ that was built by Victor Horta. It is

GAY BRUSSELS

Brussels is one of the most progressive gay culture cities in Europe. There is a concentration of gay bars, clubs and shops around rue du Marché au Charbon (D5) where people of all persuasions mix happily. A major center for information about the Brussels LGBT scene is the Rainbowhouse Bar, www.rainbowhouse.be, rue du Marché au Charbon 42, ☎ 02 503 5990. Also try www.patroc.com/brussels.

being restored and will be fully functional in 2015.

⊞ E5–6 ⊠ Rue Ravenstein 23 ☎ Box office: 02 507 8200 🕐 Box office: Mon–Sat 9–7 🚇 Parc/Park or Gare Centrale/ Centraal Station

RECYCLART

www.recyclart.be
The old train station is divided into spaces where concerts, puppet shows and other more alternative happenings are held.

⊞ D6 ⊠ Station Bruxelles-Chapelle, rue des Ursulines 25 ☎ 02 502 5734 🚇 Anneessens

THÉÂTRE 140

www.theatre140.be
Good venue for international performances of dance, drama, music and regular English-language stand-up comedy.

⊞ J4 ⊠ Avenue Eugène Plasky 140 ☎ 02 733 9708 🚋 Tram 7

THÉÂTRE NATIONAL DE LA COMMUNAUTÉ FRANÇAISE

www.theatrenational.be
The theater often arranges co-productions with Strasbourg. Most plays are in French, with a few English-speaking touring companies.

⊞ E4 ⊠ Boulevard Émile Jacqmain 111–115 ☎ 02 203 5303 🕐 Box office Mon–Sat 11–6 🚇 Rogier, De Brouckère 🚋 Tram 25, 51, 55

THÉÂTRE ROYAL DE LA MONNAIE

See page 37.

Restaurants

PRICES

Prices are approximate, based on a 3-course meal for one person.

€€€ over €45
€€ €20–€45
€ under €20

BELGA QUEEN (€€)

www.belgaqueen.be
An excellent brasserie, the Belga Queen has it all—a wonderful oyster bar with an almost endless choice, a beer bar and a cigar bar, all set in a lofty building with a huge stained-glass skylight. As the name says, everything is very Belgian, from the architecture to the refined contemporary food; beer is used in many dishes.
🚇 D4 ✉ Rue Fossé aux Loups 32 ☎ 02 217 2187 🕐 Mon–Fri 12–2.30, 7–midnight, Sat 7–midnight 🚇 De Brouckère 🚊 Tram 3, 4, 31, 32

LA BELLE MARAÎCHÈRE (€€–€€€)

www.labellemaraichere.com
This pleasant restaurant has the ambience of a country house dining room and offers excellent fish dishes with a creative flourish. Lobster soup with Armagnac and various preparations of turbot are only some of the possibilities, while even the starters are a delight.
🚇 D4 ✉ Place Ste.-Catherine 11 ☎ 02 512 9759 🕐 Fri–Tue lunch, dinner

🚇 Ste.-Catherine/St.-Katelijne 🚊 Tram 3, 4, 31, 32

BOCCONI (€€€)

www.ristorantebocconi.com
At the best Italian restaurant in town you'll find stylish decor, excellent and innovative Italian dishes and attentive but relaxed service.
🚇 E5 ✉ Hotel Amigo, rue de l'Amigo 1 ☎ 02 547 4715 🕐 Lunch, dinner 🚇 Gare Centrale/Centraal station, Bourse/Beurs

BONSOIR CLARA (€€–€€€)

www.bonsoirclara.be
This trendy brasserie-style eaterie is in a fashionable street, with a vibrant setting. Come here to enjoy excellent Mediterranean food.

RUE DES BOUCHERS

Many *Bruxellois* try to avoid the rue des Bouchers (Butchers' Street), near the Grand' Place, where at some of the restaurants *racoleurs* (hustlers) harass the passing tourists to enter their establishment. In the 1950s it was a seedy area of cabarets and cafés that doubled up as brothels. At No. 30 Petite Rue des Bouchers was the cabaret La Rose Noire, where famous Belgian singers such as Jacques Brel made their first appearances. The cabaret was demolished in 1964; the last café, Le Bourgeoys, closed in 2001.

🚇 D5 ✉ Rue Antoine Dansaert 22 ☎ 02 502 0990 🕐 Mon–Fri lunch, dinner; Sat, Sun dinner 🚇 Bourse/Beurs

LE CERCLE DES VOYAGEURS (€€)

www.lecercledesvoyageurs.com
Grand café with leather armchairs and a colonial atmosphere. The menu includes dishes from around the world and the wine list is also global.
🚇 D5 ✉ Rue des Grands Carmes 18 ☎ 02 514 3949 🕐 Daily 12–2.30, 6–10 🚇 Anneessens

COMME CHEZ SOI (€€€)

www.commechezsoi.be
The famed chef, Pierre Wynants, has retired from his signature restaurant, but Comme Chez Soi's outstanding cuisine is now in the capable and creative hands of his daughter, Laurence, and her chef husband, Lionel Rigolet. You need to reserve weeks ahead as there are only 40 seats.
🚇 D6 ✉ Place Rouppe 23 ☎ 02 512 2921 🕐 Tue, Thu–Sat 12–1, 7–9, Wed 7–9. Closed Jul 🚇 Anneessens

COMOCOMO (€€)

www.comocomo.com
A Basque *pintxo* (tapas) bar is quite something, but this restaurant takes it one step farther and has the dishes going around on a sushi conveyor belt. The style is ultra

contemporary and the food, including wild boar carpaccio, fried garlicky mushrooms and quail egg and bacon, is really good.

🔹 D5 ✉ Rue Antoine Dansaert 19 ☎ 02 503 0303 🕓 Daily 12–3, 7–11 🚇 Bourse/Beurs

DARINGMAN (€)

Old-fashioned brown café turned trendy, where the old locals meet the fashionable crowd.

🔹 D5 ✉ Rue de Flandre 37 ☎ 02 512 4323 🕓 Tue–Thu noon–1am, Fri noon–2am, Sat 4pm–2am 🚇 Ste.-Catherine/St.-Katelijne

DIVINO (€–€€)

www.divinoresto.be
Straightforward but very popular Italian restaurant with huge wood-oven baked pizzas and homemade pastas.

🔹 D5 ✉ Rue des Chartreux 56 ☎ 02 503 3909 🕓 Mon–Fri lunch, dinner; Sat, Sun dinner 🚇 Bourse/Beurs

DOMAINE DE LINTILLAC (€€)

www.restaurant-domaine-de-lintillac.be
A 1970s-style restaurant with whitewashed walls and wooden beams, red gingham table cloths and lots of candles. The food, dishes from southwest France, is excellent, with the best foie gras in town at the most reasonable prices. Excellent service and warm atmosphere.

🔹 D4 ✉ Rue de Flandre 25 ☎ 02 511 5123 🕓 Mon dinner, Tue–Sat lunch, dinner 🚇 Ste.-Catherine/St.-Katelijne

LE FALSTAFF (€–€€)

www.lefalstaff.be
At some time during an evening out everyone usually ends up at this huge but always busy art deco café with a vast terrace, heated in winter.

🔹 D5 ✉ Rue Henri Maus 19 ☎ 02 511 8789 🕓 Daily 10am–2am 🚇 Bourse/Beurs 🚋 Tram 4, 32, 55, 56

KASBAH (€€)

In a delightful dark-blue cave setting, this popular Moroccan restaurant delivers with its large menu of tajines, couscous and grills accompanied by Arabic

101 RESTAURANTS

Rue Antoine Dansaert has its fair share of trendy eateries, as does rue des Chartreux, but Brussels' ultrahip diners now head for nearby chaussée de Flandres. This street is packed with eating possibilities, from the very Belgian and excellent Viva M'Boma (▷ 46) and Le Pré Salé at No. 20, to rustic French with lots of foie gras at Le Domaine de Lintillac (▷ above). Henri at No. 113–115 is a simple but hip restaurant with fusion cuisine or you can have tea at the bookshop Bollebooks at No. 57.

music. Try the excellent Sunday brunch.

🔹 D5 ✉ Rue Antoine Dansaert 20 ☎ 02 502 4026 🕓 Mon–Fri lunch, dinner; Sat, Sun dinner 🚇 Bourse/Beurs 🚋 Tram 3, 4, 31, 32

LITTLE ASIA (€€)

www.littleasia.be
Popular, contemporary restaurant with excellent Vietnamese dishes, as well as Thai and Chinese dishes. Attentive service.

🔹 D4 ✉ Rue Ste.-Catherine 8 ☎ 02 502 8836 🕓 Mon–Sat 12–11 🚇 Bourse/Beurs 🚋 Tram 3, 4, 31, 32

LA MANUFACTURE (€€)

www.lamanufacture.be
This restaurant, in the old Delvaux leather factory, serves delicious, inventive European food with a touch of Asia. You can sit outside in summer.

🔹 C–D5 ✉ Rue Notre-Dame du Sommeil 12 ☎ 02 502 2525 🕓 Mon–Fri lunch, dinner; Sat dinner 🚇 Bourse/Beurs 🚋 Tram 3, 4, 31, 32

LE PAIN QUOTIDIEN (€)

www.lepainquotidien.com
In this chain of tea rooms, breakfast, lunch, snacks and afternoon tea are served around one big table. Try the breads, croissants, pastries and jams.

🔹 E6 ✉ Rue des Sablons 11 ☎ 02 513 5154 🕓 Daily 7.30–7 🚋 4, 95; tram 92, 93; 🔹 D5 ✉ Rue Antoine Dansaert 16 ☎ 02 502 2361

SAHBAZ (€–€€)

Slightly away from the heart of town, but this Turkish restaurant is one of the best in Brussels, and worth the small excursion. Turkish and *Bruxellois* families come here for the hearty and inexpensive kebabs, stews and delicious Turkish pizzas.

�︎ G3 ✉ Chaussée de Haecht 102 ☎ 02 217 0277 🕑 Thu–Tue 11.30–3, 6–midnight 🚋 Tram 92

SEA GRILL (€€€)

www.seagrill.be
Top chef Yves Mattagne creates high art on the plate with his superb fish dishes whose dressings and sauces do not overwhelm the main issue and are a culinary joy in their own right. Jersey scallops and king crab for starters vie with mains of sea bass, Brittany lobster or turbot on the bone, while the desserts are a perfect balance for the palate.

🚩 E4 ✉ Rue Fosse aux Loups 47 ☎ 02 212 0800 🕑 Lunch, dinner. Closed 1–5 Jan and 26 Jul–17 Aug 🚇 De Brouckère 🚋 Tram 3, 4, 31, 32

TAVERNE DU PASSAGE (€€)

www.taverne-du-passage.be
For old-time art deco Brussels, including waiters in traditional black-and-white with gold trimmings, this elegant, long-established restaurant is the place to enjoy such treats as shrimp croquettes, eels in cream and green herb sauce and mouthwatering steaks, all underpinned by one of the finest wine lists in Brussels.

🚩 E5 ✉ Galerie de la Reine 30 ☎ 02 512 3731 🕑 Daily 12–12 🚇 Gare Centrale/ Centraal Station 🚌 Bus 29, 38, 63, 71

DE ULTIEME HALLUCINATIE (€€)

www.ultiemehallucinatie.be
Worth a visit just for the art nouveau interior, but the French food is also excellent. The lamb with rosemary is delicious, as is the sole meunière and the selection of excellent pastas.

🚩 F4 ✉ Rue Royale 316 ☎ 02 217 0614 🕑 Mon–Fri lunch, dinner; Sat 6pm–11.30pm 🚇 Botanique/ Kruidtuin

STREET OF THE WORLD

Rue Antoine Dansaert has a wide variety of ethnic restaurants. Young *Bruxellois* often choose the inexpensive Vietnamese Da Kao at No. 38 for a quick bite to eat, while the trendy crowd heads for the contemporary Mediterranean cuisine of Bonsoir Clara (▷ 44) and tapas at ComoComo (▷ 44). Next door is the Moroccan Kasbah restaurant (▷ 45).

VINCENT (€€)

www.restaurantvincent.com
A real monument of Brussels cuisine, this is one of the most reliable restaurants in the area. Hunks of meat hang in the window. The dining room has hand-painted tiles and lots of character. Waiters expertly prepare dishes like steak flambée or steak tartare while you watch.

🚩 E5 ✉ Rue des Dominicains 8–10 ☎ 02 511 2607 🕑 Mon–Sat 12–2.45, 6.30–11.30, Sun 12–3, 6.30–10.30. Closed 1–11 Jan and first two weeks in Aug 🚇 De Brouckère, Gare Centrale/Centraal Station

VISMET (€€€)

Superb fish restaurant with an open kitchen, a plain wood and white-tablecloth decor but delicious fish and seafood.

🚩 D4 ✉ Place Ste.-Catherine 23 ☎ 02 218 8545 🕑 Daily 12–2.30, 7–11 🚇 Ste.-Catherine/St.-Katelijne

VIVA M'BOMA (€€€)

"Long Live My Grandma" is an absolutely delightful restaurant in an old butcher's shop, with several awards already in its pocket. It is a modest place, but the food is consistently excellent. The menu has many Belgian dishes, focusing on meat and offal.

🚩 D4 ✉ Rue de Flandre 17 ☎ 02 512 15 93 🕑 Tue–Sat 12–2.30, 7–10 🚇 Ste.-Catherine/St.-Katelijne

South of the inner ring road is a newer Brussels, with the more residential areas of Ixelles and St.-Gilles. In recent years these districts have undergone a revival, with a wealth of new shops and restaurants.

Sights   50–55

Bicycle Tour   56

Shopping   57–58

Entertainment
   and Nightlife   59

Restaurants   60–62

Top 25   TOP
                              25

Parc du Cinquantenaire
                  ▷ 50
Musée Horta ▷ 52

4

5

6
Slachthuizen en
Marchten van
Kuregem
Erasmus
Hogeschool
Brussel
Square Albert
RUE V LINTSTRAAT
CHAUSSÉE
Albert I
DE MONS
Clemenceau
Conseil
Raad
RUE DE FIENNESTRAAT
Fiennes
Bara
N D Immaculée
Bodeghem
Bodegem
Musée de la
Gueuze
Lemonnier
BOULEVARD
JAMAR

**Collégiale
des Sts-Pierre
et Guidor**
Ecole
Technique
RUE E CARPENTIER
François
Xavier

7
GARE
DU MIDI
ZUIDSTATION
Gare du Midi
Zuidstation

**Marché
du Midi**

Sint-
Zweden

Porte de Hal
Hallepoort
Musée d Folk
Hôtel des Monnaies
Munthof

RUE DES DEUX GARES
TWEESTATIONSSTRAAT

AVENUE HENRI JASPARLAAN

Louise / Louiza
N D L TOON D'OR
Stéphanie
Stefania

8
Avenue du Roi
Koningslaan
Bethléem
Bethlehem
Parvis de
Saint-Gilles
Saint-Gilles
Voorplein
Parc
Jacques
Franck
Saint
Bernard
Faider

**ST
GILLIS**

Guillaume Tell
Willem Tell
Barrière /
Barreel
**ST
GILLES**
Janson
Trinité /
Drievuldigheid
Eglise
Sainte-
Trinité

Saint Antoine
Sint Antonius
Orban
Rochefort
Combaz
Sainte Alène
Mais
Comm
Horta
Moris
Janson

9
AVENUE W CEUPPENSLAAN
Wiels
Berthelot
**Musée Horta
(Hortamuseum)**
Ma Campagne
Parc de Forest
Park van Vorst
Albert
Prison de
Saint Gilles
Gevangenis
Hotel
Hannon
ELSENE

10
Parc Duden
Dudenpark
Jupiter
Prison de Forest
Gevangenis van Vorst
Cathédrale-
Saints-Michel-
et-Gudule-
Bruxelles
Darwin
Sainte
Marie
**L'Union Saint Gilloise
Joseph Marien**
Altitude Cent
Hoogte
Honderd
Saint Augustin
Berkendael /
Berkendaal
N D Annonciation
Institute Nat
du Sang
Molière
**FOREST
VORST**
**Hôpital de
Saint Gilles**
MOLIÈRE
MOLIÈRELAAN

11
H Hart
Sacré Coeur
Vanderkindere
Institute
Médical
Ed Cavell
Churchill
Churchill
Cavell
CHURCHILL
Parc
Monti

12
Parc
Brugmann
park
**Musée David
et Alice van
Buuren**
UKKEL

0   500 m
0   500 yds

A   **B**   **C**   **D**   **E**

Arts-Loi
Kunst-Wet

Square
Frère-Orban

Saint Joseph

Maelbeek
RUE MAALBEEK DE

Berlaymont E U
U E Berlaimont

Grande
Mosquée

Ecole
Militaire
School

Dominicains

BRUXELLES-
SCHUMAN
BRUSSEL-
SCHUMAN

Pavillon
Horta

Musée Royal d'l'Armée
et d'Hist Militaire
Kon Museum v h Legeren
v d Krijgsgeschiedenis

Trône
Troon

Conseil Européen
Europese Rad

Parc du
Cinquantenaire

**Parlament Européen
(Europees Parlament)**

Quartier Européen
Europese Wijk

Brydel

Jubelpark

Parc Léopold
Leopoldspark

Musées Roy d'Art et d'Histoire
Kon Musea v Kunst

Maison
Cauchie

BRUXELLES-
LUXEMBOURG
BRUSSEL-
LUXEMBURG

Musée
d'Hist Nat

Saint
Gertrude

Place Saint-Pierre /
Sint-Pieterspleín

Musée
Wiertz

Musée des Siences
Naturelles
Musée voor Natuur-
wetenschappen

Peres du
Saint Sacrement

Acacia/
Acacias

Mais
Comm

N D Immaculée
O L V Onbevlekt

**ELSENE   Musée
d'Ixelles**

Eglise
Saint-Antoine /
Sint-Antoonkerk

De Jachel
La Chasse

ETTERBEEK

Bailli
Baljuw

Moutern /
Germon

Avt Victor Jacobsstraat

La Chasse

Dautzenberg

Lievure /
Gist

Saint
Antoine

Hôtel
Solvay

Flagey

Flagey

Hôpital
d'Etterbeek

**Avenue Louise
(Louizalaan)**

Vieurgat

Hôpital
d'Ixelles

Caserne
M Géruzet Kazerne

Caserne
Lieuten Gén
Baron de Witte
de Haelen
Kazerne

Saint
Andrew

Etterbeek Gare /
Etterbeek Station
Gendarmerie

**GARE D'ETTERBEEK
STATION ETTERBEEK**

Abbaye
Abdij

Saint Philippe
de Néri

Prêtres du
Sacré-Cœur

N D de
la Cambre

IXELLES

**Musée Constantin
Meunier**

Buyl

Jeanne /
Johanna

Place de la
Petite

Legrand

Cambre-Etoile /
Ter Kamerenster

Bascule

**Stade de
l'ULB**

ULB

BRUSSEL

ULB
VUB

stitute Médico-
Chirurgical
Longchamp

Longchamp

*Bois de
la Cambre*

N D du
Saint Rosaire

F   G   H   J

Parc du Cinquantenaire

HIGHLIGHTS

● Treasure Room at the Musée du Cinquantenaire
● Pavillon Horta-Lambeaux
● Views over the city from the top of the triumphal arch

DID YOU KNOW?

● Maison Cauchie, at rue des Francs 5 (open first weekend each month 10–1, 2–5.30, Tue (Jun–Aug) 6–9pm, www.cauchie.be), is the finest example of art nouveau architecture in Brussels. Paul Cauchie, who built the house in 1905, was a sgraffito painter.

Built to celebrate 50 years of Belgian independence, this park has all you would imagine in the way of grand buildings—even its own grand jubilee arch. It also has some surprises.

The most famous city park In 1880, Leopold II ordered the building of the Palais du Cinquantenaire, with two huge halls, to hold the National Exhibition in the park. For the next 25 years, the king dreamed about erecting a monumental arch. It was finally built in 1905 by Charles Girault, with two colonnades added in 1918.

Remarkable monuments Several features here recall important international fairs. An Arab-inspired building, which housed a panorama of Cairo in an 1897 fair, is now Brussels' Grand Mosque.

Clockwise from top left: vintage cars at Autoworld; enjoying the Montgomery fountain in nearby avenue de Tervuren; silhouette of the Arc du Cinquantenaire; a shining exhibit at Autoworld; red Ferrari cars line up in front of the Arc du Cinquantenaire; remembering a bygone era at Autoworld

The Pavillon Horta-Lambeaux (currently closed in part for renovation, inquire at Tourist Information offices for opening hours) was erected in 1889 to designs by Victor Horta to house the *haut-relief* of the *Human Passions*, by Jef Lambeaux.

Grand but dusty museums One of the National Exhibition halls now showcases Autoworld, a prestigious collection of vintage cars from 1886 to the 1970s. The Musée Royal de l'Armée et d'Histoire Militaire incorporates an aviation museum, with planes displayed in a huge hangar, and houses weapons from medieval times to the present. The rich Musée du Cinquantenaire, in the south wing of the Palais du Cinquantenaire, has items from ancient civilizations, Belgian archaeological discoveries and important European decorative arts and lace.

THE BASICS

+ H–J6
- ✉ Main entrances rue de la Loi and avenue du Chevalier
- 🚇 Merode, Schuman
- 🚌 22, 27, 61, 80; tram 81

Autoworld
www.autoworld.be
- ☎ 02 736 4165
- 🕐 10–6 (until 5, Oct–Mar)
- 🍴 Café
- ♿ Good ✋ Moderate

Musée Royal de l'Armée et d'Histoire Militaire
www.klm-mra.be
- ☎ 02 737 7811
- 🕐 Tue–Fri 9–5, Sat, Sun 10–6
- 🍴 Café
- ♿ Good ✋ Free

Musée du Cinquantenaire
www.kmkg-mrah.be
- ☎ 02 741 7211
- 🕐 Tue–Fri 9.30–5, Sat, Sun 10–5
- ♿ Good ✋ Moderate

Musée Horta

Many of the grand buildings designed by architect Victor Horta have been destroyed, but here in his house, on the rue Américaine, the flowing lines and the play of light and space clarify his vision.

New style Victor Horta (1861–1947) built these two houses on the rue Américaine as his home and studio between 1898 and 1901. Now a museum, they illustrate the break he made from traditional town houses, with their large, gloomy rooms. Horta's are spacious and airy, full of mirrors, white tiles and stained-glass windows. A light shaft in the middle of the house illuminates a banister so gracious and flowing that you just want to slide down it. The attention to detail in the house is amazing, even down to the last door handle, all designed in fluid art nouveau style.

The Horta Museum (left); the Brussels Comic Strip Museum designed by Horta (below)

Art nouveau in St.-Gilles There are other interesting properties in residential St.-Gilles. Strolling around the area between rue Defacqz and St.-Gilles Prison you can admire several examples of art nouveau style, dating from the late 19th to early 20th centuries. Paul Hankar designed the Ciamberlani and Janssens mansions at rue Defacqz 48 and 50, and his own house at No. 71. One of the most beautiful art nouveau facades in Brussels, designed by Albert Roosenboom, is at rue Faider 85. At rue de Livourne 83 you can see the private house of the architect Octave Van Rysselberghe, who also built the Otlet mansion at rue de Livourne 48. The Hannon mansion, built at avenue 1 de la Jonction by Jules Brunfaut, is now a photographer's gallery; look for the impressive fresco by Paul-Albert Baudouin in the staircase.

THE BASICS

www.hortamuseum.be

🔢 E9

✉ Rue Américaine, St.-Gilles 25

☎ 02 543 0490

🕐 Tue–Sun 2–5.30

🚌 54; tram 81, 91, 97 from place Louise

♿ Few

Ⓜ Moderate

❓ Guidebooks and guided tours are available

More to See

AVENUE LOUISE

Avenue Louise is one of the places where you'll see *Bruxellois* heading for the designer boutiques. The avenue, and the trendy Ixelles district, are where Brussels bureaucrats come to spend their money; they crowd the many smart cafés, spilling onto the streets, and part with hundreds of euros in its stores. It is one of Brussels' main shopping areas, with boutiques, interior designers, showrooms, art galleries, hotels and restaurants.

➕ E–F–G7–10 ✉ Avenue Louise
🍽 Restaurants nearby 🚇 Louise/Louiza
🚌 38, 54, 60; tram 93, 94 ♿ Good

BOIS DE LA CAMBRE

Once part of the Forest of Soignes, this green area was annexed by the city in 1862 and laid out in 1869 by landscape artist Edouard Keilig. Boating, bicycling, fishing and roller-skating are among the activities on offer here.

➕ G11–G12 ✉ Main entrance on avenue Louise ⏰ Dawn–dusk 🚌 Tram 25, 94
♿ Few 💲 Free

COLLÉGIALE DES STS. PIERRE ET GUIDON

The Romanesque crypt dates from the 11th century, but the superb Gothic church, with frescoes, is from the 14th to 16th centuries. The altar is illuminated by light filtering through the lovely stained-glass window above. The rare Celtic tombstone is believed to mark the grave of St. Guidon.

➕ Off A7–A8 ✉ Place de la Vaillance
☎ 02 523 0220 ⏰ Daily 9–12, 2–5; services Mon–Thu 8.45am, Fri 6pm, Sat 4.30pm, Sun 5pm. Closed during services 🚇 St.-Guidon/St.-Guido ♿ Few 💲 Free

EUROPEAN PARLIAMENT

The imposing facade of the European Parliament building, made of slick granite, glass and steel, is nicknamed the Caprice des Dieux (whim of the gods). This is where the European Union's MEPs gather when in Brussels.

➕ G6 ✉ Rue Wiertz 60 ☎ 02 284 2111
⏰ Audio-guided visits Jul–Aug Mon–Thu 10, 11, 2, 3, Fri 10, 11; Sep–Jun Mon–Thu 10, 3, Fri 10 🚇 Schuman ♿ Good 💲 Free

Striking architecture in the European Parliament district

MARCHÉ DU MIDI

The Marché du Midi is one of Europe's largest markets, with fresh fruit and vegetables, fish, meat, clothes, pictures, household goods, North African music and books.

🚹 C7 ✉ Near Gare du Midi 🕐 Sun 6–1.30 🚇 Gare du Midi/Zuidstation 🚌 Tram 3, 4, 31, 32, 51, 81, 82, 83 🚹 Few 🎫 Free

MUSÉE D'IXELLES

www.museumofixelles.irisnet.be

Since the 1800s, Ixelles/Elsene has attracted Belgian intellectuals, artists and writers, so a museum of 19th- and 20th-century Belgian art comes as no surprise. Housed in an old slaughterhouse, the collection includes works by Auguste Rodin, who had a studio in the area. What attracts the crowds are the temporary exhibitions of modern art and architecture.

🚹 G8 ✉ 71 rue Jean Van Volsem 71 ☎ 02 515 64 21 🕐 Tue–Sun 9.30–5 🚌 38, 59, 60, 71; tram 81 🎫 Free (moderate for temporary exhibitions) 🚹 Moderate wheelchair access

MUSÉE CONSTANTIN MEUNIER

www.fine-arts-museum.be

This museum is dedicated to the life and works of painter and sculptor Constantin Meunier (1831–1905), with more than 150 of his works in what was once his house and studio. Meunier was disturbed by the hard living conditions of the working class, and became famous for his paintings and sculptures of suffering workers.

🚹 F10 ✉ 59 rue de l'Abbaye ☎ 02 648 4449 🕐 Tue–Fri 10–12, 1–5 🚇 Louise 🚌 Tram 93, 94 🎫 Free 🚹 Difficult

MUSÉE DAVID ET ALICE VAN BUUREN

www.museumvanbuuren.com

This delightful museum is in the van Buurens' elegant art deco house. The interior and the gardens are stunning, and the art collection of the banker and his wife is equally remarkable, including Brueghel and Van Gogh.

🚹 E12 ✉ Avenue Léo Errera 41 ☎ 02 343 4851 🕐 Wed–Mon 2–5.30 🚌 Tram 3, 4, 7 🚹 Few wheelchair facilities 🎫 Moderate

Brussels is the political heart of Europe

Art Nouveau Bicycling Tour

Brussels has a wealth of art nouveau architecture. This tour takes in works by two of the main players, Victor Horta and Paul Hankar.

DISTANCE: 4km (2.5 miles) **ALLOW:** 2 hours

START

HÔTEL SOLVAY, AVENUE LOUISE 224
🚇 F8–9 🚋 Louise, then tram 94

END

PLACE LOUISE
🚇 E7 🚋 Louise

❶ Start at the fine Hôtel Solvay, built by Victor Horta in 1898. Cycle northwest along avenue Louise and take the third street to the left, rue Paul-Émile Janson. Here you'll see the Hôtel Tassel at No. 6, which was built by Horta in 1893.

❷ Turn right on rue Faider and then left onto rue Defacqz. No. 48 is a house by Paul Hankar, and No. 51 is his studio. Turn left on rue Simonis to place du Châtelain, with lots of cafés. Continue on rue du Page to rue Américaine and take a right to the Musée Horta (▷ 52–53).

❸ Continue along the street and take a left on chaussée de Charleroi. No. 55 is the remarkable art nouveau house Les Hiboux (the Owls) and next door is the superb Hôtel Hannon, built in 1903 and now a photo gallery.

❹ From adjoining avenue Brugmann take a right on rue Félix Delhasse, with two smaller art nouveau houses at Nos. 13–15. Go right on rue de la Glacière, left on chaussée de Waterloo and right onto avenue Ducpétiaux. Nos. 13, 15 and 47 are by Paul Hankar.

❽ Take a right onto rue Jourdan and continue to place Louise.

❼ Take a left on rue du Métal and then turn right on rue de l'Hôtel des Monnaies, with, at No. 66, Hôtel Winssinger, by Horta (1894).

❻ Turn right on rue Maurice Wilmotte and left on rue d'Irlande to place L. Morichar. Turn right on rue de Roumanie, left on rue de la Croix de St.-Pierre, with (Nos. 76, 78 and 80) more houses by Paul Hankar.

❺ There are art nouveau houses by lesser-known architects all along the way back. Take a left on rue du Portugal, then right on rue Moris, and left again on rue d'Espagne.

Shopping

ART DECO 1920–1940
www.artdecoannebastin.be
After admiring Brussels' amazing art deco and art nouveau facades, you may want to see some period furniture, and that is just what this shop specializes in. Equally impressive is the collection of art deco jewelry.
🚹 D9 ✉ Avenue Adolphe Demeur 16, St.-Gilles
☎ 02 534 7025 🕙 Thu–Mon 11–6.30 🚋 Tram 3, 4, 51, 81, 83, 97

BALTAZAR
www.baltazar.be
Whether you're in the market for an original by Pierre Alechinsky or some other modern artist, or a more modest litho from some other big name, you might well find it here. Some sculptures are displayed in the garden at the back of the house.
🚹 E10 ✉ Avenue du Haut Pont 5 (at Avenue Brugmann)
☎ 02 512 8513 🕙 By appointment only 🚋 Tram 92

BEER MANIA
www.beermania.be
Here you'll find the largest selection of beers in town, with more than 400 types, from the most obvious to some rare ones. You can also buy the correct glasses for your preferred beer, sample beers in the back of the shop or attend classes or tasting sessions.
🚹 F7 ✉ Chaussée de Wavre 174–176 ☎ 02 512 1788

🕙 Mon–Sun 11–8 🚇 Porte de Namur/Naamsepoort

CHURCH'S
www.church-footwear.com
If the name of this retailer sounds otherworldly, it's appropriate to the heavenly experience of wearing their handmade English shoes. Each pair takes up to 10 weeks in the making.
🚹 E7 ✉ Place Stéphanie 2
☎ 02 512 4430 🕙 Mon–Sat 9.30–6.30 🚋 Tram 92, 93, 94, 97

DE CONINCK
www.deconinckwine.com
Founded in 1886 in Waterloo, the firm is now in its fourth generation as a family business specializing in fine wines, primarily from France, where they have their

> #### MATONGÉ
> Matongé takes its name from an area in Kinshasha, in the Democratic Republic of Congo, the former Belgian Congo, and it's by far the city's most exotic district. At its heart is the Galerie d'Ixelles, between chaussées Wavre and d'Ixelles. It sells African beauty products, foods, fashion and music. The pedestrian rue Longue Vie has several lively African bars and restaurants. At the split of the two chaussées is a wonderful giant mosaic by the Zairean artist Chéri Samba, worth the excursion.

own vignoble. The Ixelles branch is a trove of noble wines.
🚹 H12 ✉ Avenue du Pesage 1 ☎ 02 640 4465
🕙 Tue–Fri 11–1, 1.30–7, Sat 10.30–1, 1.30–7
🚋 Tram 25, 94

LE DÉPÔT D'IXELLES
www.depotbd.com
Le Dépôt d'Ixelles is a good place to find the latest comic strips, secondhand comic strips, books, video games and music.
🚹 F7 ✉ Chaussée d'Ixelles 120 ☎ 02 511 7504
🕙 Tue–Sat 11–6.30 🚇 Porte de Namur/Naamsepoort
🚋 54, 71

LES ENFANTS D'EDOUARD
www.lesenfantsdedouard.com
From Ralph Lauren and Gucci to Belgium's Olivier Strelli to Stella McCartney, this eclectic and delightfully eccentric shop deals in good condition, second-hand high fashion.
🚹 E8 ✉ Avenue Louise 175
☎ 02 640 4245 🕙 Mon–Sat 10–6.30 🚇 Louise/Louiza
🚋 Tram 93, 94

HÔTEL DES VENTES VANDERKINDERE
www.vanderkindere.com
This expensive auction house specializes in art and objects from the 17th and 18th centuries.
🚹 D9 ✉ Chaussée d'Alsemberg 685–687, St.-Gilles ☎ 02 344 5446
🕙 Mon–Fri 9–12, 2–5. Phone for times of sale 🚋 Tram 51

HUNTING & COLLECTING

www.huntingandcollecting.com
This top fashion salon offers exciting clothing styles, also perfume, fashion media and cool ceramics. Designer labels include Givenchy, Kenzo and top Belgian designers such as Christian Wijnants.
🗺 D5 ✉ Rue des Chartreux 17 ☎ 02 512 7477 🕐 Tue–Sat 12–7 🚇 Bourse/Beurs 🚌 46; tram 3, 4, 31, 32

IDEB LIFESTORE

www.ideb.be
This is a wonderful and luxurious department store in a grand house with sweeping stairways. It is where the *Ixellois* hang out on the weekends to shop for the latest carefully selected fashion for men, women and the house, as well as beauty products and books. When you have finished shopping, take a break in the restaurant, bar or beauty room.
🗺 E7 ✉ Boulevard de Waterloo 49 ☎ 02 289 1110 🕐 Mon–Fri 10.30–7, Sat 11–7 🚇 Louise/Louiza

LOOK 50

The oldest vintage store in Brussels has an excellent selection of secondhand clothes and accessories from the 1950s to 1980s. All are at very reasonable prices. In the same street are several other vintage stores, as well as other quaint little boutiques.
🗺 F7 ✉ Rue de la Paix 10 ☎ 02 512 2418 🕐 Mon–Sat 10.30–6.30 🚇 Porte de Namur/ Naamsepoort

MARCHÉ PLACE DU CHÂTELAIN

This delightful square has a good selection of restaurants and bars that are perfect for a lunch stop and is one of the liveliest people-watching spots in Brussels. On Wednesday afternoons, between 2pm and 7pm, food-lovers flock here for the city's best food market, with fine charcuterie, cheeses, homemade jams, wines and delicious pastries.
🗺 E–F9 ✉ Place du Châtelain 🕐 Wed 2–7 🚌 Tram 92

NATAN COUTURE

The upscale fashions on display at this imposing mansion store, one of a small chain in Belgium and close-by countries, change seasonally but tend to emphasize an elegant and subtle femininity.
🗺 E8 ✉ Avenue Louise 158 ☎ 02 647 1001 🕐 Mon–Sat 10–6 🚌 Tram 93, 94

SENTEURS D'AILLEURS

www.senteursdailleurs.com
A sumptuous boutique with a selection of the perfumes, home fragrances and skincare items made by perfumers who don't cater to the mass market. Needless to say, the shop smells divine and has a totally relaxing atmosphere. If the choice is too overwhelming, the staff are all experts who trained as "noses" and can assist in finding something that suits you to perfection.
🗺 F8 ✉ Place Stéphanie 1A (off avenue Louise) ☎ 02 511 6969 🕐 Mon–Sat 10–6.30 🚇 Louise/Louiza 🚌 Tram 94

SERNEELS

www.serneels.be
A spacious shop with a wonderful, but expensive, range of traditional and contemporary toys, from tiny ducklings to full-size cars and fine rocking horses. There is also a range of games and pastimes for older children.
🗺 E8 ✉ Avenue Louise 69 ☎ 02 538 3066 🕐 Mon–Fri 9.30–6.30 🚇 Louise/Louiza 🚌 Tram 94

QUARTIER DU CHÂTELAIN

The quiet streets and elegant art nouveau houses in this district attract a young crowd, and the area around place du Châtelain is fast becoming a trendy shopping hub. There is a picturesque food market on Wednesday afternoons on the square, and some trendy restaurants and interesting fashion boutiques have opened in the streets adjoining the square, such as rue de l'Aqueduc, rue Simonis, rue du Page and rue Faider.

Entertainment and Nightlife

CHEZ MOEDER LAMBIC

www.moederlambic.com
With some 400 Belgian beers to choose, you're sure to find something to your taste in this jewel of Belgian bars. On warm summer evenings you can imbibe outside at a table on the street.

➕ D9 ✉ Rue de Savoie 68 ☎ 02 544 1699 🕐 Daily 4pm–3am 🚇 Lombardie 🚋 Tram 81

CLUB AVENUE

www.clubavenue.be
Belgium's star DJs appear at this funky venue, in the upper town, with a low-key setting and a glamorous crowd. Thursday's "Stardust Nights" are free, and on Sundays they have "Funky Fever Evenings."

➕ E7 ✉ Avenue de la Toison d'Or 44 ✉ Thu–Sat from 10.30pm 🚇 Louise/Louiza or Porte de Namur/Naamsepoort

FLAGEY

www.flagey.be
Wonderful arts venue in the old art deco-style state TV buildings, shaped like a cruise liner, which often has performances of jazz or world music. Also has Brussels' most comfortable cinema, showing classic films.

➕ G8 ✉ Place Eugène Flagey, Ixelles ☎ 02 641 1020 🚋 38, 59, 60, 71; tram 81, 83

FOREST NATIONAL

www.forestnational.be
One of Belgium's largest venues draws many major bands and stars, despite the bad acoustics and endless parking problems.

➕ B12 ✉ Avenue Victor Rousseau 208 ☎ 02 340 2123 🚋 48, 54; tram 32, 82, 97

SOUNDS JAZZ CLUB

www.soundsjazzclub.be
Great jazz café regularly featuring the best international and local jazz musicians. Near place Ferdinand Lecocq, which is stocked with good bars.

➕ F7 ✉ Rue de la Tulipe 28, Ixelles ☎ 02 512 9250 🕐 Mon–Sat 8pm–4am 🚇 Porte de Namur/Naamsepoort 🚋 34, 38, 54, 71

LA SOUPAPE

www.lasoupape.be
In its homey nook close to les Étangs d'Ixelles this small bar-theater puts on a steady diet of *chanson française*, lovingly presented and performed.

➕ G9 ✉ Rue Alphonse de Witte ☎ 02 649 5888 🚋 38, 59, 60, 71; tram 81, 82

STYX

www.styx.cinenews.be
A small repertory cinema with films in the original language, often English.

➕ F7–8 ✉ Rue de l'Arbre Bénit 72, Ixelles ☎ 02 512 2102 🚇 Porte de Namur/Naamsepoort

LE TAVERNIER

www.le-tavernier.be
This lively bar has a huge terrace area and indoor space, but it can often be hard to find a place to sit. Most of the regulars tend to hang out at the bar, or dance the early hours away on weekends.

➕ G8–9 ✉ Chaussée de Boondael 445 ☎ 0475 241 523 🕐 Daily 11am–early morning 🚋 Tram 81, 82

THÉÂTRE DE POCHE

www.poche.be
Occupying an exceptional, leafy site at the north end of the Bois de la Cambre, the "Pocket Theater" focuses on socially committed performance—though not to the extent of being unwilling to indulge in laughter—most of it in French.

➕ G11 ✉ Chemin de Gymnase 1a (reached from avenue Legrand) ☎ 02 649 1727 🚋 Tram 7, 93, 94

BELGIUM DANCES

Belgium's reputation for contemporary dance has flourished since the late Maurice Béjart founded his Ballet du XXe Siècle and the Mudra school in 1953—and revolutionized dance in the country. There are now more than 50 companies in residence in Brussels, most of them very contemporary. Anne Teresa De Keersmaeker and her company, Rosas, are the resident troupe at the city's Théâtre Royal de la Monnaie, and regularly perform around the world.

Restaurants

PRICES

Prices are approximate, based on a 3-course meal for one person.
€€€ over €45
€€ €20–€45
€ under €20

AU VIEUX BRUXELLES (€€)

www.auvieuxbruxelles.com
Founded in 1882, this place virtually oozes old-fashioned Bruxellois charm and quality. Diners pile in to sample its trademark multifarious moules (mussels) specialties, along with the other seafood and local dishes on the menu. Polished wood paneling and classic red-checked tablecloths set the tone inside.
🕂 F7 ⊠ Rue St.-Boniface 35 ☎ 02 503 3111 🕓 Daily dinner 🚇 Porte de Namur/ Naamsepoort 🚊 54, 71

AUX MILLE ET UNE NUITS (€€)

www.milleetunenuits.be
This Tunisian restaurant stands out in an area packed with North-African eateries. Inside, it is an interpretation of a tent in the desert, with fairy lights replacing the stars in the sky. The food, from the salads and little pies to the couscous with lamb and onions, is delicious.
🕂 D8 ⊠ Rue de Moscou 7 ☎ 02 537 4127 🕓 Mon–Sat 12–3, 6–11.30 🚇 Porte de Hal/Hallepoort 🚊 Tram 3, 4, 51

BRASSERIE VERSCHUEREN (€)

This archetypal Brussels brown café has art deco touches and a great beer selection. It attracts lots of regulars.
🕂 D8 ⊠ Parvis de St.-Gilles 11 ☎ 02 539 4068 🕓 Daily 11am–2am or later 🚊 Tram 3, 4, 51

CAFÉ BELGA (€)

www.cafebelga.be
Huge bar-restaurant in the old cruise-liner-shape television building (▷ 59) overlooking the lake in Ixelles. The large terrace is a good place for breakfast, or a drink before a movie. Or you can watch the passers-by and even the ducks on the lake.
🕂 G8 ⊠ Place Eugène Flagey 18 ☎ 02 640 3508 🕓 Open 24 hours 🚊 38, 71; tram 81, 83

ST.-BONIFACE

The picturesque art nouveau district of St.-Boniface is flourishing again after too many years of neglect. Focused around the church and the well-established l'Ultime Atome (▷ 62) are now several trendy eateries, including the excellent French brasserie Saint-Boniface and Citizen (hot Thai and Vietnamese food). Most places have terraces on the pretty square, so it's a great place to sit on a nice day.

CHEZ MARIE (€€–€€€)

This trendy one-Michelin-star restaurant serves delectable French-Belgian food. The wine list is one of the city's finest and the two-course lunch is good value.
🕂 G9 ⊠ 40 rue Alphonse de Witte ☎ 02 644 3031 🕓 Tue–Fri lunch, dinner; Sat dinner 🚊 71; tram 81

LE CLAN DES BELGES (€€)

www.leclandesbelges.com
In this contemporary Belgian restaurant you can sample the country's traditional fare with an elegant modern twist. The setting is hip and the prices moderate.
🕂 F7 ⊠ Rue de la Paix 20 ☎ 02 511 1121 🕓 Mon–Fri lunch, Sat, Sun dinner 🚇 Porte de Namur/ Naamsepoort

LE FILS DE JULES (€€)

www.filsdejules.be
Popular Basque restaurant serving delicious cuisine from southwest France in a very stylish setting. Also has a good wine list. Reservations are essential.
🕂 E9 ⊠ 37 rue du Page ☎ 02 534 0057 🕓 Mon–Fri, 7pm–11pm, Sat, Sun 7pm–midnight 🚊 54; tram 81

LE FRAMBOISIER DORÉ (€)

The most delicious sorbets in town, homemade in the traditional way, and with a wealth of tastes, including

speculoos, the Belgian version of gingerbread.
➕ F9 ✉ Rue du Bailli 35 ☎ 02 647 5144 🕐 Daily 12–8 🚌 54; tram 81, 83

GIOCONDA STORE CONVIVIO (€–€€)

A lively restaurant attached to an Italian wine and delicatessen store, serving tasty pasta dishes. The waiters are friendly and entertaining.
➕ E9 ✉ Rue de l'Aqueduc 76 ☎ 02 539 3299 🕐 Mon–Sat lunch, dinner 🚌 54; tram 81

LE HASARD DES CHOSES (€€)

Lively and deservedly popular Mediterranean restaurant serving big plates of tasty salads and pastas. The decor is simple but attractive and the terrace at the back is open in summer.
➕ E9 ✉ Rue du Page 31 ☎ 02 538 1863 🕐 Daily 12–11 🚌 54; tram 81, 83

L'HORLOGE DU SUD (€–€€)

www.horlogedusud.be
Lively West African restaurant with Congolese and Senegalese dishes, which include a lot of fish, yams and vegetables. Enjoy exotic cocktails with names such as "Life is Good" and "Sunny Mood."
➕ F–G7 ✉ Rue du Trône 141 ☎ 02 512 1864 🕐 Mon–Fri 11–3, 6–midnight, Sat 6pm–midnight 🚇 Trône/Troon 🚌 38, 95

MAISON ANTOINE (€)

www.maisonantoine.be
Generally regarded as the best *frietkot* in Brussels, a stall with cones of delicious "Belgian" fries and a wide range of sauces and meaty accompaniments, which are allowed to be consumed in the cafés around the square.
➕ H7 ✉ Place Jourdan ☎ 02 230 5456 🕐 Sun–Thu 11.30am–1am, Fri–Sat 11.30am–2am 🚌 59, 60, 80

LA QUINCAILLERIE (€€€)

www.quincaillerie.be
An elegant and delightful restaurant in an old hardware store, a short

VEGETARIAN CHOICE

Although meat is popular among Belgians, vegetarians shouldn't find it too difficult to get something tasty to eat. Specifically vegetarian restaurants in Brussels include L'Elément Terre (✉ 465 chaussée de Waterloo, Ixelles ☎ 02 649 37 27); La Tsampa (✉ 109 rue de Livourne, Ixelles ☎ 02 647 0367), a Tibetan health food restaurant; Shanti (✉ avenue Adolphe Buyl 68 ☎ 02 649 4096), which serves seafood as well as purely vegetarian dishes; and Den Teepot (✉ rue des Chartreux 66 ☎ 02 511 9402), a lunch-only vegan place.

walk from the Horta Museum (▷ 52). La Quincaillerie specializes in fish and seafood, serving huge platters of seafood, but you'll also find other delights of the Belgian and French kitchen.
➕ E9 ✉ Rue du Page 45 ☎ 02 533 9833 🕐 Mon–Sat lunch, dinner; Sun dinner only 🚌 54; tram 81, 83

ROUGE TOMATE (€€€)

www.rougetomate.be
Classical elegance balanced by contemporary design complement the subtle and delicious food at this popular restaurant. Vegetarian dishes are to the fore and the wine list is selected by one of the best French *sommeliers*.
➕ F8 ✉ Avenue Louise 190 ☎ 02 647 7044 🕐 Mon–Fri lunch, dinner, Sat dinner 🚌 54; tram 81, 83

L'ULTIME ATOME (€€)

www.ultimeatome.com
A brasserie that is both trendy and traditional, with a large variety of beers and other drinks, simple but good Belgian dishes and long opening hours. Very popular on weekends, when locals come for breakfast and lunch. Enjoy a coffee on the terrace when the sun shines on this atmospheric little square.
➕ F7 ✉ Rue St-Boniface 14 ☎ 02 513 4884 🕐 Mon–Fri 8am–12.30am, Fri, Sat 9am–1am, Sun 10am–12.30am 🚇 Porte de Namur/Naamsepoort

Bruges

Bruges never fails to impress, with its romantic canals, quaint cobbled streets, medieval facades, bridges and towers and amazing collection of Flemish masters.

Sights	66–86

Walk	87

Shopping	88–89

Entertainment and Nightlife	90

Restaurants	91–92

Top 25   **TOP 25**

Begijnhof ▷ 66
Burg ▷ 68
Canal Cruise ▷ 70
Choco-Story ▷ 71
Groeninge Museum ▷ 72
Gruuthuse Museum ▷ 74
Kathedraal St.-Salvator ▷ 75
Markt ▷ 76
Onze-Lieve-Vrouwekerk ▷ 78
St.-Janshospitaal en Memling Museum ▷ 80
De Vesten en Poorten ▷ 82

WARANDEBRUG
Handelskom

Brandweer
Komvest
ST-LEONAR-
DUSBRUG
Sasplein

Wulpenstr

Museum Onze-Lieve-
Vrouw ter Potterie

O L Vrouw van de
Potterie Kerk

BUITEN
KRUISVEST

Oost-Proosse

Peterseliestraat

Bisschoppelijk
Seminarie

Ollebaan

Hotel-en Toerisme-
school Spermalie

Kazerne

St-Janshuismolen

Snaggaardstraat

Engels
Klooster

Guido
Gezelle-
museum

Carmersstraat

Rolweg

Museum voor
Volkskunde

Kant-
centrum

Verrieststr

Schuttersgilde
Sint-Joris

Jeruzalemkerk

Kruispoort

Sint-Annakerk

Peperstraat

Sint-
Walburgkerk

LANGESTR

Gerechtshof

HOOGSTR

KRUISPOORTBRUG

silliek van het
lig-Bloed

LANGESTR

Balsemboomstr

markt

Rijkswacht

BUITEN KAZERNEVEST

Predikherenstr

Koningin-
Astridpark

St-Magda-
lenakerk

Capaardstr

Gentpoor

Willemijnendreef

BUITEN BONINVEST

GENTPOORTBRUG

Centpoortvest

BUITEN GENTPOORTVEST

Bruges

c   d

Begijnhof

HIGHLIGHTS

● The courtyard
● Statue of Our Lady of Spermalie
● *Béguine's* house

TIPS

● The courtyard is particularly beautiful in early spring, abloom with daffodils.
● Next to the Begijnhof is the equally picturesque Minnewater (▷ 85), the so-called Lovers' Lake, lined with trees.

A haven of tranquility, the fine enclosed courtyard of the Begijnhof is one of the oldest in Belgium, and one of Bruges' most picturesque corners.

Closed court From the 12th century onward, single or widowed pious women started living together in communities, often after losing their men to the Crusades. They took vows of obedience to God and spent their days praying and making lace for a living. Their cottages were built around a courtyard and surrounded by walls. There were many of these *Begijnhoven* *(Béguinages)*, but the one in Bruges is the best preserved. Since 1927, the Bruges Begijnhof has been occupied by Benedictine nuns, whose severe black-and-white habits are a reminder of those of the *béguines* who once lived there.

A statue of Our Lady sits on the facade of the Begijnhof (left) and spring flowers brighten the lawn (below)

The church Several times a day the nuns walk to the church through the green garden at the side of the square. The simple church (1605) is dedicated to St. Elisabeth of Hungary, whose portrait hangs above the entrance. She also appears in a painting by Bruges master Lodewijk de Deyster (1656–1711). The most important work is the statue of Our Lady of Spermalie (c.1240), the oldest statue of the Virgin in Bruges. On the left wall as you face the altar is a superb statue of Our Lady of Good Will. The remarkable alabaster sculpture of the Lamentation of Christ at the High Altar dates from the early 17th century.

A *béguine's* house The tiny museum near the gate, a reconstruction of a 17th-century *béguine's* house, complete with furniture and household goods, gives an idea of how this community lived.

THE BASICS

✚ b4
✉ Wijngaardplein
☎ 050 33 00 11
🕐 Church and Begijnhof daily 6.30–6.30. Museum Mar–Nov Mon–Sat 10–12, 1.45–5.30 (Jul–Aug to 6pm), Sun 10.45–12, 1.45–5; Dec–Feb Wed, Thu 11–12, 1.45–4.15
🚌 1, 11
♿ Good
💲 Free. Museum inexpensive

Burg

HIGHLIGHTS

● Gotische Zaal in the
Stadhuis
● Stadhuis facade
● Mantelpiece of Charles V
in Brugse Vrije museum
● Basiliek van het Heilig-
Bloed (▷ 83)
● Toyo Ito's Architectural
Pavilion

TIP

● Admire the square at
night, when the crowds
have gone.

**This historic enclave evokes medieval
Bruges better than any other part of
the city. Its impressive buildings once
contained the offices of the church, city,
county and judicial authorities.**

A separate entity Until the 18th century, the
Burg was walled in and locked with four gates.
The north side of the square was dominated by
the 10th-century St. Donatian's Church, sold by
auction and torn down soon after in 1799.
(Under the trees, there is a scale model of the
church, and some of its foundations can be seen
in the basement of the Holiday Inn hotel.)

The square The whole of the square's west side
was once the Steen, an impressive 11th-century
tower; only the porch beside the stairs to the

Clockwise, from top left: Bruges' Town Hall is the oldest in Belgium; visitors enjoy a horse-and-cart tour of the Burg; ornate carvings decorate the buildings surrounding the historic square

Basiliek van het Heilig-Bloed (▷ 83) remains. To the southeast is the Flemish-Renaissance Civiele Griffie (Civil Recorders' House 1535–37). On the square's east side is the early 18th-century version of the Landhuis van het Brugse Vrije, the one-time seat of government of the Vrije, an autonomous rural and coastal region of the medieval period. Inside the palace is the *Mantelpiece of Charles V*, a Renaissance work of art by Lancelot Blondeel.

Stadhuis Built between 1376 and 1420, Bruges' town hall is the oldest in Belgium. Although its turreted sandstone facade dates from 1376, the statues on its Gothic facade date from the 1970s. The Gotische Zaal (Gothic Room) is where Duke Philip the Good called together the first States General of the Ancient Low Countries in 1464; it is now reserved for private functions.

THE BASICS

➕ C3
✉ Burg
🕐 Town Hall (Gothic Room): daily 9.30–5.
Museum: Brugse Vrije daily 9.30–12.30, 1.30–5
🍴 Restaurants nearby
🚌 All buses to the Markt
♿ Very good
💶 Inexpensive
❓ Concerts in summer

Canal Cruise

TOP 25

Take a relaxing canal cruise within Bruges (left) or a longer trip to Damme (below)

THE BASICS

Departure points: Rozenhoedkaai, Nieuwstraat, Huidenvettersplein, Wollestraat, Katelijnestraat

Generally March–Nov 10–6; also during the Christmas period in mild weather and some evening cruises in summer

Moderate

HIGHLIGHTS

● Groenerei
● Meebrug
● The smallest window in Bruges at the Gruuthuse Museum (▷ 74)
● Views of the Onze-Lieve-Vrouwekerk (▷ 78)

TIPS

● Illuminated evening tours, offered in summer, are particularly pleasant.
● There is a flea market along the Dijver on Sunday in summer.
● For a longer canal trip, take the boat to Damme (▷ 96–97).

Bruges is often referred to as "the Venice of the North" and its reien (as the Brugeans call their canals) provide much of the city's romantic charm. Taking a boat on the canals is also one of the best ways to explore the heart of Bruges.

Where to start Several companies offer the same canal cruise that can be picked up from various departure points, including the Vismarkt (on Huidenvettersplein) and Dijver (on Nieuwstraat and Wollestraat). Commentary is given in several languages. There are regular departures, as the boats fill up, throughout the day (see the side panel for when the boats run).

Highlights to spot The view of the Groenerei/Steenhouwersdijk seen from the Vismarkt is one of the most idyllic (and often painted) scenes in Bruges. The Meebrug and the Peerdenbrug are two of the city's oldest stone bridges. At the end of Groenerei is the Godshuis (Almshouse) de Pelikaan. Rozenhoedkaai is another wonderful corner, with rear views of the buildings of the Burg and Huidenvettersplein and of the Duc de Bourgogne hotel. Along the Dijver are some of Bruges' grandest buildings, including the Gruuthuse Museum (▷ 74) and Onze-Lieve-Vrouwekerk (▷ 78). The canal becomes much more intimate after that and has several wooden medieval houses, before it ends at the Begijnhof (▷ 66), just before the Minnewater (▷ 85), which was the outer port of Bruges before the river silted up, cutting the city off from the sea.

Choco-Story

Bruges is famous for its many chocolate shops, but this chocolate museum tells you all you ever needed to know about this delicious product, from the history of cocoa to the production of the famous Belgian pralines.

Chocolate history The museum is housed in the grand 15th-century Maison De Croon, an old wine tavern and later a pastry bakery. The first part of the museum evokes 2,500 years of chocolate history, through an impressive and well-explained collection of more than 1,000 objects illustrating the origins and evolution of chocolate. The earliest finds date from 600BC, when traces of cocoa were found in terra-cotta pots used by the Mayas of Colha (now in Belize, Central America), who were believed to drink their hot chocolate with a lot of foam. In 1519 the conquistadores discovered America and also the cocoa drink, which during the 17th and 18th centuries becomes increasingly popular with the European royals and aristocracy. Only much later was chocolate eaten as a confectionery bar.

Pralines and tastings The museum also explains how chocolate is made, with particular attention to the differences in ingredients and production processes over the years. At the end of the visit there is a demonstration of how the pralines are made, and how the fillings are inserted with care. To round off the visit there is a tasting of the freshly made chocolates, and you can ask the expert chocolate-maker about his secrets.

THE BASICS

www.choco-story.be
🏠 c2–3
✉ St.-Jansstraat 7B (St.-Jansplein)
☎ 050 61 22 37
🕐 Daily 10–5 (closed some days in Jan)
🚌 4, 14, 43
♿ Moderate

HIGHLIGHTS

● *Chocolateros*, 19th-century ceramic vases with a pouring lip and a tube for blowing air into the chocolate to create foam
● Maison De Croon
● Chocolate tasting

BRUGES TOP 25

71

Groeninge Museum

HIGHLIGHTS

● *Madonna with Canon Joris van der Paele*, van Eyck
● *Moreel Triptych* and *Annunciation*, Hans Memling
● *Portrait of a Brugean Family*, Jacob van Oost
● *The Assault*, René Magritte

TIP

● You can buy a combination ticket for €15 that gives entrance to either five museums of your choice (except privately owned museums) or to three museums including bike rental and a drink.

Jan van Eyck's serene *Portrait of Margaretha van Eyck* and Gerard David's gruesome *Judgment of Cambyses*, portraying a magistrate being skinned alive, are so arresting that it is easy to overlook the contemporary art found in this impressive museum.

The Flemish Primitives The 15th-century Flemish Primitives were so named in the 19th century to express a desire to recapture the pre-Renaissance simplicity in art. Room 1 shows works by van Eyck (*c.*1390–1441), including the *Portrait of Margaretha van Eyck*, the painter's wife. There are two works by Hans Memling— the *Moreel Triptych* and two panels of *The Annunciation*—as well as works by Rogier van der Weyden, Hugo van der Goes and the last

Admiring the art (below left); an oil painting by Jordaens (below)

of the Flemish Primitives, Gerard David, including his *Judgment of Cambyses.* In Room 7, the 16th-century works of Pieter Pourbus illustrate the Italian influence on Flemish style. In Room 8, look for the lovely baroque *Portrait of a Brugean Family* by Jacob van Oost (1601–71).

Modern Flemish masters Emile Claus (1849–1924) and Rik Wouters (1882–1916) are well represented. Also look for works by James Ensor, Gust de Smet, Gustave van de Woestijne and Rik Slabbinck; works by Constant Permeke represent the best of Flemish Expressionism. There are two paintings by Paul Delvaux and one by René Magritte. The last room shows works by Brugeans Luc Peire and Gilbert Swimberghe, and Roger Raveel and also contains a cabinet by avant-garde artist Marcel Broodthaers (1924–75).

THE BASICS

✚ c3
✉ Dijver 12
☎ 050 44 87 11
🕐 Tue–Sun 9.30–5
🍴 Cafeteria
🚌 1, 11
♿ Good
✋ Moderate

73

Gruuthuse Museum

The museum's eye-catching emblem outside, and porcelain and tapestries inside

THE BASICS

➕ b3
✉ Dijver 17
☎ 050 44 87 11
🕐 Tue–Sun 9.30–5
🚌 1
♿ None
💶 Moderate; Brangwyn Museum inexpensive

HIGHLIGHTS

● Sculpture rooms
● Prayer balcony
● Gombault and Macée Tapestry series
● Illuminated courtyard at night
● Smallest window in Bruges, seen from the Boniface Bridge
● Views from loggia over Reie, Boniface Bridge and Onze-Lieve-Vrouwekerk

The facade and peaceful courtyard of the Gruuthuse Palace take you back to medieval times. It is a delight to stroll around the nearby Arentspark and watch boats glide under the Boniface Bridge, one of Bruges' most romantic corners.

The palace of Gruuthuse Built in the late 15th century by the humanist and arts lover Lodewijk van Gruuthuse, this medieval palace now houses the Gruuthuse Museum, a fascinating collection of antiques and applied arts, well laid out in a series of 22 numbered rooms. There are some fine sculptures, including an early 16th-century Gothic kneeling angel rendered in oak; the impressive *Christ, Man of Sorrows* (c.1500), and the 15th-century *Reading Madonna* by Adriaan van Wezel.

Brugean tapestries Well-preserved 17th-century examples in the Tapestry Room represent the *Seven Liberal Arts*; and some fine baroque wool and silk counterparts in Room 8 have pastoral themes, including the excellent comic-strip-like tapestry the *Country Meal*. Room 16 is the prayer room, in the form of a balcony that looks down into the Onze-Lieve-Vrouwekerk (▷ 78), one of the oldest parts of the building.

Brangwyn Museum (Arents Huis) The Arents House, opposite the coach house, is home to the Brangwyn Museum. Here you'll find the world's largest collection of work by Frank Brangwyn (1867–1956), a British artist born in Bruges.

Kathedraal St.-Salvator

One of the cathedral's Brussels tapestries (below); looking to the high altar (right)

The Kathedraal St.-Salvator, together with the belfry and the Onze-Lieve-Vrouwekerk, towers above Bruges. The splendid sculptures and tapestries inside are a reminder of the cathedral's long and eventful history.

The cathedral A house of prayer existed here as early as the 9th century; it was dedicated to St. Saviour and to St. Eloi, who is believed to have founded an earlier wooden church here in 660. The present cathedral was built near the end of the 13th century. It was damaged by several fires, and in 1798 many of its treasures were stolen by the French, who put the building and its contents up for auction the following year. However, wealthy Brugeans bought a lot back. The neo-Romanesque top was added to the remarkable tower in 1844–46 and the spire in 1871. The oldest sections of the tower date back to 1127.

Sculptures and tapestries The large statue of *God the Father* (1682) by Artus Quellinus is one of the best baroque sculptures in Bruges. The doors of the Shoemakers' chapel, as well as the sculptures in the Cross chapel and the Peter and Paul chapel, are superb examples of late Gothic oak carving. Six of the eight 18th-century tapestries in the choir and transept, illustrating the life of Christ, were woven in Brussels.

The museum There are wonderful pieces of 15th-century Flemish art among the 120 paintings in the museum, as well as gold and manuscripts.

THE BASICS

+ b3
- Zuidzandstraat
- 050 33 68 41
- Mon–Sat 10–1, 2–5.30, Sun 11.30–12, 2–5. Museum Sun–Fri 2–5
- All city buses
- Very good
- Cathedral free; museum inexpensive

HIGHLIGHTS

- *Martyr's Death of St. Hippolytus*, Dirk Bouts' triptych (1470–75)
- *Last Supper*, Pieter Pourbus
- 14th-century *Tanner's Panel*
- *The Mother of Sorrows*
- Baroque statue of *God the Father*
- Eekhout Cross in Shoemakers' chapel
- Eight tapestries by Jasper van der Borght

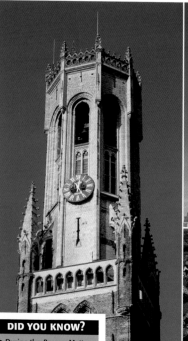

DID YOU KNOW?

● During the *Brugse Metten* massacre (18 May 1302), Flemish workers and citizens killed hundreds of occupying French soldiers.

● The statue of Jan Breydel and Pieter de Coninck was unveiled three times.

● The Belfry tower is 83m (272ft) high, has 366 steps to the top and leans southeast.

● The tower has a four-octave carillon of 47 bells cast by Joris Dumery in 1748.

● The combined weight of the bells is 27 tons.

● The carillon marks the quarter hour.

The Belfort (Belfry), emblematic of Bruges' medieval power and freedom, dominates the city's main square, the Markt (Market). The square is ringed with Gothic and neo-Gothic buildings.

The city's core This square, with its attractive historic buildings, has always been at the heart of Bruges. A weekly market was held here from 1200 until it was moved to 't Zand in 1983. The Central Post Office (1887–1921) and the 19th-century neo-Gothic Provinciaal Hof (Provincial Government Palace) stand on the site of the former Waterhallen, a huge covered dock. Across Sint-Amandstraat is Craenenburg House, where Maximilian of Austria was locked up in 1488. The square's north side was once lined with tilers' and fishmongers' guildhalls, which are now restaurants.

The Belfry (far left) towers over Bruges' Markt. Climb its 366 steps for wonderful views over the square

Heroes There is a bronze statue (1887) of two medieval Bruges heroes, Jan Breydel and Pieter de Coninck, who in 1302 led the *Brugse Metten*, the massacre of hundreds of occupying French soldiers by Flemish workers. The same year saw the rebellion of the Flemish against the French king, Philip IV, culminate at the Battle of the Golden Spurs, resulting in Flanders' independence.

The Hallen and Belfry The origins of the Hallen (town hall and treasury) and the Belfry (called the Belfort or Halletoren in Bruges) go back to the 13th century, when the Hallen were originally the seat of the municipality and the city's treasury. From the balcony, the bailiff read the "Hallen commands," while the bells warned citizens of approaching danger or enemies. Now you can enjoy carillon concerts here throughout the year.

THE BASICS

- b3
- Markt
- ☎ 050 44 87 11
- ⏱ Belfry daily 9.30–5
- 🍴 Restaurants and tea rooms nearby
- 🚌 All city buses
- 🎫 Belfry moderate
- ❓ Carillon concerts all year Wed, Sat, Sun 11am, mid-Jun to mid-Sep, Mon and Wed 9pm

Onze-Lieve-Vrouwekerk

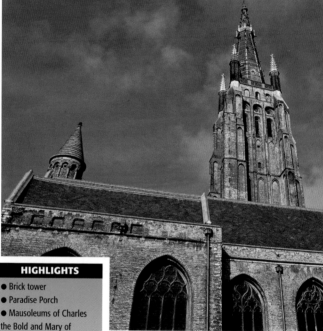

HIGHLIGHTS

- Brick tower
- Paradise Porch
- Mausoleums of Charles the Bold and Mary of Burgundy
- *Madonna and Child*, Michelangelo
- *The Adoration of the Shepherds*, Pieter Pourbus
- *Our Lady of the Seven Sorrows*, probably by Adriaen Isenbrandt
- *The Transfiguration of Mount Tabor*, Gerard David

TIP

- Attend a church service in the Onze-Lieve-Vrouwekerk. The acoustics are excellent, and your eyes can linger on the great Gothic architecture.

Beneath the monumental brick tower in the Church of our Lady, the religious feeling is palpable, heightened by the aroma of incense, the magnificent sculptures and the stunning paintings all around you.

One of Bruges' seven wonders Although there was a chapel here about 1,000 years ago, the choir and facade on Mariastraat date from the 13th century, and the aisles and superbly restored Paradise Porch from the 14th and 15th centuries. The church's most striking feature is the tower, 122m (400ft) high, begun in the 13th century.

Artworks The star attraction is the *Madonna and Child* by Michelangelo (1475–1564). Other sculptures include a rococo pulpit (1743) by the Bruges painter Jan Garemijn, some fine altars

The Church of our Lady (left) dates from the 13th century. Inside, see Michelangelo's Madonna and Child (below)

and the Lanchals monument in the Lanchals chapel (15th century). The prayer balcony connected to the Gruuthuse mansion (▷ 74) enabled the lords of Gruuthuse to attend services directly from home. The church contains some important 16th-century Flemish paintings, including works by Gerard David, Pieter Pourbus and Adriaen Isenbrandt. The valuable *Katte of Beversluys*, a jewel-encrusted monstrance weighing 3kg (7lb), is kept in the sacristy.

Mausoleums Both Charles the Bold, who died in 1477, and Mary of Burgundy, who died in 1482 after a hunting fall, are buried here in superb adjacent mausoleums, moved to the Lanchals chapel in 1806 and returned here in 1979. Excavations revealed beautiful 16th-century frescoes in other tombs.

THE BASICS

✚ b3
✉ Mariastraat
🕐 Mon–Sat 9.30–4.30, Sun 12–4.30; no sightseeing during church services
🚌 1
♿ Very good
💰 Inexpensive
❓ Weekend services: Sat 5 and 6.30pm, Sun 11am

St.-Janshospitaal en Memling Museum

DID YOU KNOW?

● On the back of *The Mystical Marriage of St. Catherine*, Memling painted the donors.

● Jan Florein donated *The Adoration of the Magi*, and is shown kneeling on the left of the painting.

● Adriaan Reins, friar of the hospital, is on the side panel of *The Lamentation of Christ.*

The Hans Memling works on show here are 15th-century landmarks in the history of art and are not to be missed. The building that houses them is also a gem.

The hospital St. John's, founded in the 12th century, is one of Europe's oldest hospices (medieval hospitals) and continued until 1976, when medical care was moved to a new building. The Gothic Maria Portal (c.1270) on Mariastraat is the original gate. Subsequent buildings include a tower, central ward, brewery, monastery, bathhouse, cemetery (all 14th century), St. Cornelius Chapel (15th century) and a convent for the hospital's sisters (1539). The 17th-century dispensary, with exhibits of remedies, and the church are particularly interesting. The wards were renovated in 2001 and some were converted into cafés and shops.

The Memling Museum was once a medieval hospital

The Memling masterpieces As St. John's reputation as a hospital grew, so did its wealth. Its funds were invested, with inspiration, in the works of Hans Memling, a German painter who had settled in Bruges by 1465 and died one of its richest citizens in 1494. Four of the six works on display here were commissioned by St. John's friars and sisters, the most famous being the *Ursula Shrine* (1489), a reliquary in the shape of a church, gilded and painted with scenes from the life of St. Ursula. The triptych *Mystical Marriage of St. Catherine* (1479) was commissioned for the chapel's main altar, as were two smaller triptychs—*The Adoration of the Magi* (1479) and *The Lamentation of Christ* (1480). The diptych *Madonna with Child* (1487) and the portrait of *The Sibylla Sambetha* (1480) were moved here from the former St. Julian's hospice in 1815.

THE BASICS

- ✚ b3
- ✉ Mariastraat 38
- ☎ 050 44 87 11
- 🕐 Tue–Sun 9.30–5
- 🚋 1
- 🍴 Restaurants nearby
- ♿ Very good
- 💰 Moderate

De Vesten en Poorten

The round towers of the medieval Gentpoort

THE BASICS

✚ Gentpoort c–d4;
Kruispoort d3;
Smedenpoort a3;
Ezelpoort b2

TIPS

● The ramparts of Bruges (6.5km/4 miles long) were laid out as parks in the 19th century and are ideal for a good jogging session or pleasant walk.
● Alternatively, rent a bicycle (▷ 118) as there are cycling routes all along.

DID YOU KNOW?

● The statue of St. Adrian (1448, remodeled in 1956) on Gentpoort was carved by Jan van Cutsegem to ward off plague.
● Smedenpoort's bronze skull (hung there in 1911) replaces the real skull of a traitor.
● There were 25 windmills in Bruges in 1562.

To understand Bruges' layout, take a bicycle ride or walk around its walls, especially on the east side, where the gates, ramparts, windmills and canals give the impression of containing the city, as they have done for 600 years.

Fortified Bruges Bruges' original fortifications (de Vesten en Poorten) date back to ad1000, but nothing survives of the six original bastion gates beyond an inscription on Blinde Ezelstraat marking the location of the south gate. Between 1297 and 1300, as the medieval city grew increasingly wealthy, new defenses were built; of the seven new gates, four survive, two in the east—Kruispoort (Cross Gate, 1402), with a drawbridge, and Gentpoort (Ghent Gate, 14th century) with twin towers—and two in the west—Bruges' only two-way gate, Smedenpoort (Blacksmiths' Gate, 14th century) and Ezelpoort (Donkeys' Gate, rebuilt in the 17th and 18th centuries).

Blowing in the wind The eastern ramparts were used as raised platforms for windmills, but only four mills remain between Kruispoort and Dampoort. The first mill when viewed coming from Kruispoort, Bonne Chiere (Good Show), was built in 1888 and reconstructed in 1911, but has never worked. The second, St.-Janshuismolen (St. John's House Mill; ▷ 86), near the junction of Kruisvest and Rolweg, was built by bakers in 1770. The third, De Nieuwe Papegaai (New Parrot), a 1790 oil mill, was moved to Bruges from Beveren in 1970. A fourth, built in the 1990s, is near the Dampoort.

More to See

BASILIEK VAN HET HEILIG-BLOED
www.holyblood.com

This is a double chapel, with the 12th-century Romanesque St.-Basilius Chapel downstairs, shrouded in mystery and rich with the atmosphere of the Middle Ages. Even visitors who are casual about religion tend to fall silent in the face of the intense devotion of some of the worshipers. The Reliquary of the Holy Blood is kept in the upstairs 19th-century neo-Gothic chapel. The crystal phial containing two drops of holy blood is contained in a gold and silver reliquary, richly decorated with pearls and precious stones. One of the holiest relics of medieval Europe, it is believed to have been brought here by Thierry d'Alsace, who was given it by the Patriarch of Jerusalem during the Second Crusade. It is believed that at first the blood in the phial liquefied every Friday, a miracle that stopped in the 15th century, but the chapel is still opened on Friday for the worship of the Holy Blood. The reliquary is carried around the city every year during the Procession of the Holy Blood. The museum contains paintings, tapestries and other silver reliquaries.

🚇 c3 ✉ 10 Burg ⏰ Apr–Sep daily 9.30–12, 2–5; Oct–Mar daily 10–12, 2–4. Closed Wed afternoon and during services 🚌 All buses to the Markt ♿ None 💰 Inexpensive ❓ Sun services 11am. Worship of the Holy Blood Wed 10–11am

BROUWERIJ DE HALVE MAAN
www.halvemaan.be

De Halve Maan is the only family brewery still working in the heart of Bruges and it's been running since 1856. A tour takes about 45 minutes, after which you can try the delicious local Brugse Zot (Mad Bruges) beer.

🚇 b4 ✉ Walplein 26 ☎ 050 44 42 22 ⏰ Apr–Oct Sun–Fri 11–4 Sat 11–5 every hour; Nov–Mar Mon–Fri 11 and 3, Sat, Sun 11–4 every hour 🚌 1, 2 💰 Moderate

CONCERTGEBOUW
www.concertgebouw.be

Finished in 2002 to celebrate Bruges as the European City of Culture, this

Looking down on 't Zand from the Concertgebouw

The annual Procession of the Holy Blood

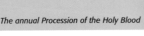

BRUGES MORE TO SEE

impressive structure has already become the city's fourth landmark. It has the largest stage in Belgium, and attracts international performances.
b3 't Zand 050 47 69 99
During performances All city buses

DIAMANTMUSEUM

www.diamondmuseum.be
This private museum tells the history of Bruges as the oldest diamond hub in Europe. The art of diamond polishing was invented in the 15th century by the local goldsmith Lodewijk van Berquem. Diamonds are one of Belgium's main export products and the museum features the imaginary workshop of Lodewijk van Berquem, a replica of the crown of Margaret of York made in Bruges, mining equipment and diamond manufacturing tools used in Belgium, and thousands of real diamonds. A daily polishing demonstration takes place at 12.15 in the museum's workshop.
b–c4 Katelijnestraat 43 050 34 20 56 Daily 10.30–5.30. Closed middle 2 weeks Jan 1

JAN VAN EYCKPLEIN

Standing at the heart of this picturesque square is a statue of the famous Flemish painter Jan van Eyck. At No. 2 is the old Tolhuis (Toll House), where the ships coming into Bruges' inner port had to pay taxes on their cargo. It is now an information office. The square overlooks the beautiful Spiegelrei, with some of the city's grandest houses on the canal. In the nearby square of the Woensdagmarkt is a statue of another Flemish Primitive painter, Hans Memling.
c2 Jan van Eyckplein 6 Free

JERUZALEMKERK

The plan for this 15th-century church was inspired by the Basilica of the Holy Sepulcher in Jerusalem. The remarkable interior includes fine stained-glass windows and the tomb of the Genoese merchant Anselmus Adornes and his wife, who built the almshouses next to the church. Half of the original 12 almshouses have survived.

Learn how people made a living in days gone by at the Museum voor Volkskunde

✚ c–d2 ✉ Peperstraat 3a 🕐 Mon–Fri 10–12, 2–6, Sat 10–12, 2–5. Closed holidays 🚌 6, 16 ♿ Good 💷 Inexpensive

KONINGIN ASTRIDPARK

This green zone in the heart of the city is laid out in 18th-century English country style, with a good selection of trees, a pond and a pleasant children's playground.

✚ c3 ✉ Main entrance Park 🕐 24 hours 🚌 1, 11 ♿ Good 💷 Free

MINNEWATER

South of the Begijnhof (▷ 66) is the Minnewater—the Lovers' Lake. This was the outer port before the river silted up and cut Bruges off from the sea. It is named after a woman called Minna who, according to legend, fell in love with a man her father did not like. Minna hid in the woods around the lake, and died there before her lover could rescue her. Her lover parted the waters and buried her under the lake. Next to the lake is a delightful park, with a sculpture garden and free concerts in summer.

✚ b4 ✉ Arsenaalstraat 🕐 Dawn–dusk 🍴 Café-restaurant 🚌 All buses to train station ♿ Good 💷 Free

MUSEUM ONZE-LIEVE-VROUW TER POTTERIE

This wonderful little museum is in a former hospital dating from the 13th to 17th centuries. There are sculptures, 15th- and 16th-century paintings, tapestries and furniture. The church has one of Bruges' finest baroque interiors.

✚ c1 ✉ Potterierei 79 ☎ 050 44 87 11 🕐 Tue–Sun 9.30–12.30, 1.30–5 🚌 4, 14, 43 ♿ Very good 💷 Inexpensive

MUSEUM VOOR VOLKSKUNDE

Bruges' past is recalled in these beautifully restored 17th-century almshouses, originally built for shoemakers. Period rooms, including an old pharmacy, a shoemaker's workshop and a small sugar bakery, give an insight into the traditional professions. You can also see the costumes people wore and learn about the popular worship. After

The beautiful St.-Jakobskerk (▷ 86), founded in the 13th century

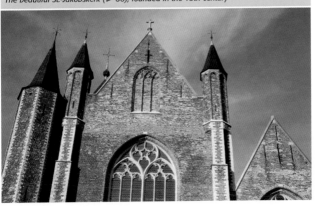

the visit, have a rest in the traditional inn "De Zwarte Kat."

➕ c2 ✉ Balstraat 43 ☎ 050 44 87 11 🕐 Tue–Sun 9.30–5 🍴 Medieval inn De Zwarte Kat 🚌 6, 16 ♿ Good 💷 Inexpensive

ST.-JAKOBSKERK

This beautiful church was founded c.1240 in a district of rich Brugean families and foreign delegations, who all made generous donations for the decoration of the building. The church has a rich collection of paintings by Pieter Pourbus, Lancelot Blondeel and several anonymous Flemish Primitives.

➕ b2 ✉ Sint-Jakobsplein 1 ☎ 050 33 18 34 🕐 Apr–Sep daily 10–1, 2–6 🚌 3, 13

ST.-JANSHUISMOLEN

The only one of Bruges' four windmills that can be visited, St.-Janshuismolen was built by a group of bakers in 1770 and acquired by the city of Bruges in 1914. It still grinds grain in summer. Inside is a museum.

➕ d2 ✉ Kruisvest ☎ 050 44 87 11

🕐 May–Sep Tue–Sun 9.30–12, 1.30–4.30 🚌 6, 16 ♿ None 💷 Inexpensive

SINT-WALBURGAKERK

Jesuit Pieter Huyssens built this splendid baroque church between 1619 and 1642, and the 17th-century oak pulpit is astonishing. In summer the church is open to the public at night, with special lighting and music. Another fine feature of this building are the white communion rails, which are almost waxlike in appearance.

➕ c2 ✉ Sint-Maartensplein 🕐 Daily 2–5pm 🚌 6, 16 ♿ None 💷 Free

VISMARKT

The fish market was built in 1821 and North Sea and Atlantic Ocean fish and seafood is still sold here from Tuesday to Saturday. The market has a few good fish restaurants, and shops where you can pick up a *stokvis* (dried fish eaten as a snack) or *maatje* (cured herring served with onions).

➕ c3 🕐 Market daily morning 🚌 All buses to the Markt 💷 Free

A view over the canal from the Vismarkt

Lesser-known Bruges

Discover the canals and quiet medieval streets of this less-touristy corner of Bruges, with its low houses and beautiful churches.

DISTANCE: 2km (1.2 miles) **ALLOW:** 2 hours

START

SINT-WALBURGAKERK
✚ c2 🚌 6, 16

END

BURG
✚ c3 🚌 All buses to Markt

❶ Start at Boomgaardstraat, with the baroque church of St. Walburga (▷ 86). Turn right onto Hoornstraat, then right on Verwersdijk.

❽ At the end of the street is Vismarkt (▷ 86), with its fish market. To the right, an alley under the arch leads to the Burg (▷ 68).

❷ Cross the bridge and walk along St.-Annakerkstraat to Jeruzalemstraat, with the Jeruzalemkerk (▷ 84), with its unique, and often macabre, artifacts beckoning to the right.

❼ Before the end of Langestraat turn left onto Predikherenstraat, just past the bridge, and turn right to Groenerei, one of Bruges' loveliest corners.

❸ Walk along Balstraat, with the Museum voor Volkskunde (▷ 85). Cross Rolweg to Carmersstraat and turn right.

❻ On the corner with Rolweg is a museum dedicated to the Flemish poet Guido Gezelle (1830–99) and farther along, the Bonne Chiere windmill. At the Kruispoort, turn right onto Langestraat.

❹ No. 85 is the English convent; No. 174 is the old Schuttersgilde St.-Sebastiaan, the archers' guildhouse; and straight ahead on Kruisvest is the St.-Janshuis windmill (▷ 86).

❺ Take a right along Kruisvest.

BRUGES WALK

87

Shopping

'T APOSTELIENTJE

This small shop offers professional advice about lacemaking. You can buy the tools you need to make lace, along with ready-made old and modern lace.

✚ c2 ✉ Balstraat 11 ☎ 050 33 78 60 🕓 Mon–Sat 9.30–6, Sun 11–4 🚌 6, 16

BAZAR BIZAR

www.bazarbizar.be
Plenty of decorative objects, gifts and jewelry imported from all over the world.

✚ b2 ✉ St.-Jakobstraat 3/5 ☎ 050 33 80 16 🕓 Mon–Sat 10.30–6 🚌 3, 13

BOEKHANDEL RAAKLIJN

www.boekhandelraaklijn.be
A good range of foreign-language books, especially paperbacks and art books.

✚ b3 ✉ Kuipersstraat 1 ☎ 050 33 67 20 🕓 Mon–Sat 9–6 🚌 3, 13

THE BOTTLE SHOP

www.thebottleshop.eu
You enter a cornucopia of beer, bottles and glasses in this emporium just off the Markt. Many of the hundreds of beers on offer are Belgian, including lambic and gueuze beers, and lots of the highly individual glasses that go with them.

✚ c3 ✉ Wollestraat 13 ☎ 050 34 99 80 🕓 Daily 9am–11pm (summer), Wed–Mon 9am–7pm (winter) 🚌 All buses to Markt

BRUGS DIAMANTHUIS

www.diamandhouse.net
The technique of diamond polishing is attributed to the mid-15th-century Bruges goldsmith van Berquem, and Bruges was Europe's first diamond city. This shop offers a large selection of quality diamonds and diamond jewelry. See also the Diamantmuseum (▷ 84).

✚ c4 ✉ Cordoeaniersstraat 5 ☎ 050 34 41 60 🕓 Daily 10.30–5.30 🚌 6, 16

CHOCOLATIER DEPLA POL

www.poldepla.be
This shop sells some of the city's finest handmade chocolates, particu-

---

FABRICS AND LACE

In the 13th century, Belgium was already famous for woven fabrics and intricate tapestries, made from English wool and exported as far as Asia. By the 16th century, Brussels was renowned for the fine quality of its lace. Lace remains one of the most popular traditional souvenirs of Brussels and Bruges but few Belgian women learn the craft today. As a result, there is not enough handmade lace to meet the demand, and what there is has become very expensive. Many shops now sell lace made in China, which costs less but is inferior.

---

larly truffles, florentines and marzipan.

✚ b3 ✉ Mariastraat 20 ☎ 050 34 74 12 🕓 Daily 10–6 🚌 1

DELDYCKE

www.deldycke.de
A quality deli with Belgian specials as well as the best foods from around the world.

✚ c3 ✉ Wollestraat 23 ☎ 050 33 43 35 🕓 Wed–Mon 9–6.30 🚌 All buses to Markt

DIKSMUIDS BOTERHUIS

www.diksmuidsboterhuis.be
The oldest cheese shop in Bruges with hams and sausages hanging from the ceiling, and a superb selection of Belgian and French cheeses and breads.

✚ b3 ✉ Geldmuntstraat 23 ☎ 050 33 32 43 🕓 Mon–Sat 10–12.30, 2–6.30 🚌 All buses to Markt

DILLE & KAMILLE

www.dille-kamille.be
A wonderful shop with simple white household ware, herbs and spices, wooden toys and cake moulds.

✚ b3 ✉ Simon Stevinplein 17–18 ☎ 050 34 11 80 🕓 Mon–Sat 9.30–6.30 🚌 All city buses

L'HEROÏNE

www.lheroine.be
The best selection of Belgian fashion is found at this small but excellent store, stocking Dries Van

Noten, Kaat Tilley, Chris Janssens and younger Belgians such as Frieda Degeyter.

🚩 b3 ✉ Noordzandstraat 32 ☎ 050 33 56 57 🕐 Mon–Sat 10–6 🚌 All city buses

HOET OPTIEK
www.hoet.be
Funky optician with spectacles 'to be seen in'.

🚩 b2–3 ✉ Vlamingstraat 19 ☎ 050 33 50 02 🕐 Mon–Fri 9–6.30, Sat 9–6 🚌 All buses

KANTCENTRUM (LACE CENTRE)
www.kantcentrum.com
See historical exhibits or watch an afternoon lace-making demonstration. Lacemaking materials are on sale.

🚩 d2 ✉ Balstraat 16 ☎ 050 33 00 72 🕐 Mon–Sat 10–4.30. Lacemaking demonstrations Mon–Sat 2–5 💷 Inexpensive 🚌 6, 16

MALESHERBES
Small shop specializing in French wines, foie gras from Périgord in France, homemade terrines and farmhouse cheeses. Next door is a small bistro.

🚩 b4 ✉ Stoofstraat 5 ☎ 050 33 69 24 🕐 Wed–Sun from 6pm 🚌 1

MASSIMO DUTTI
www.massimodutti.com
A high-end and ultra-chic fashion brand for menswear and womenswear, also children.

🚩 b3 ✉ Zuidzandstraat 41 ☎ 050 34 40 38 🕐 Mon–Fri 10–5, Sat 10–6.30 🚌 1, 3, 4

THE OLD CURIOSITY SHOP
This tiny shop has a very large collection of old postcards, posters, secondhand books and old photographs.

🚩 b4 ✉ Walstraat 8 ☎ 050 34 35 91 🕐 Tue–Sun 2–6.30 🚌 1, 11

OLIVIER STRELLI
www.strelli.be
A branch of the Brussels' fashion store.

🚩 b3 ✉ Eiermarkt 3 ☎ 050 34 38 37 🕐 Mon–Sat 10–6 🚌 All buses to Markt

DE REYGHERE
www.dereyghere.be
Books in Flemish, French, English and German, and international newspapers and magazines.

🚩 b3 ✉ Markt 12 ☎ 050 33 34 03 🕐 Mon–Sat 8.30– 6.15 🚌 All buses to Markt

ROMBAUX
www.rombaux.be
Lovely old-fashioned store with sheet music, CDs and instruments.

🚩 c3 ✉ Mallebergplaats 13 ☎ 050 33 25 75 🕐 Mon

BELGIAN COOKIES

Pain à la Grècque is a light crispy cookie covered in tiny bits of sugar, while *speculoos* is a finer version of gingerbread. The *couque de Dinant* is a hard, bread-like cookie that comes in beautiful shapes—windmills, rabbits, peasants, cars and more.

2–6.30, Tue–Fri 10–12.30, 2–6.30, Sat 10–6 🚌 All buses to Markt

SERVAAS VAN MULLEM
Excellent chocolatier and patisserie, and a great place to sample the best pastries in town.

🚩 b2–3 ✉ Vlamingstraat 56 ☎ 050 33 05 15 🕐 Wed–Sun 7.30–6 🚌 3, 13

SPEGELAERE
Bruges' best kept secret: all chocolates are made on site; the house special is a bunch of grapes made from marzipan covered in black chocolate. Don't miss the famous "Bruges Cobblestones."

🚩 b2 ✉ Ezelstraat 92 ☎ 050 33 60 52 🕐 Tue–Sat 8.30–12, 1–6.30, Sun 9–1 🚌 3, 13

DE STRIEP
www.striepclub.be
De Striep specializes in comic strips, mainly Belgian and French, but some English.

🚩 c4 ✉ Katelijnestraat 42 ☎ 050 33 71 12 🕐 Tue–Sat 10–12, 1.30–7, Mon 1.30–7, 1st Sun of the month 2–6 🚌 1

YANNICK DE HONDT
Stylish antiques shop with a mix of 15th- to 18th-century European and Japanese furniture and African art.

🚩 b3 ✉ Mariastraat 12 ☎ 050 34 51 46 🕐 Mon–Sat 2–6 🚌 All city buses

Entertainment and Nightlife

CACTUS CLUB
www.cactusmusic.be
The main venue in town for rock, jazz and world music, with the Cactus Club@MaZ seating 400 people, and the Cactus@MaZ with standing room for 1,000. The Cactus Club also organizes an open-air festival in Minnewaterpark during the second weekend of July, as well as other summer festivals in several central locations in Bruges.
🔒 a3 ✉ MaZ, Magdalenastraat 27, Sint-Andries ☎ 050 33 20 14 🚌 25

CONCERTGEBOUW
www.concertgebouw.be
Opened in 2002, the Concertgebouw aims to attract the best international and national performers in its large and perfectly equipped performance halls (▷ 83).
🔒 b3 ✉ 't Zand 34 ☎ 050 47 69 99/070 22 33 02 (ticket line) 🚌 All buses to 't Zand

CULTUURCENTRUM
www.cultuurcentrumbrugge.be
Seven venues under one name are here, including the renovated Stadsschouwburg (▷ this page) and MaZ, a new platform for youth culture. The performances in all these venues include contemporary dance, world music, drama, comedy and classical music concerts,

as well as a range of exhibitions.
🔒 b3 ✉ St.-Jacobsstraat 20–26 ☎ 050 44 30 40. Box office: 050 44 30 60
🎭 Box office: Mon–Fri 10–1, 2–6, Sat 10–1 🚌 All city buses

ENTRENOUS
www.bauhauszaal.be
A centrally located club that captures the Bruges zeitgeist with a range of top DJs and themed party nights. It caters to a young crowd without being exclusive.
🔒 d2 ✉ Langestraat 145 ☎ 050 34 10 93 🎭 Fri–Sat 10pm–late 🚌 6, 16

KINEPOLIS BRUGGE
Kinepolis is the newest and largest cinema complex in town and has eight cinemas showing mainly original versions of Hollywood blockbusters.
🔒 Off map at a4 ✉ Koning Albert 1-laan 200, Sint-Michiels ☎ 050 30 50 00 🚌 27

LIBERTY
Mainstream films in their subtitled original

version are shown at this cinema.
🔒 b3 ✉ Kuipersstraat 23 ☎ 050 33 20 11 🚌 3, 13

LUMIÈRE
www.lumiere.be
The Theatre De Korre's two cinema screens feature mainly foreign art-house films and better Belgian productions, without popcorn or advertising. Part of the complex is De Republiek (▷ 92), a café that is hugely popular with locals.
🔒 b2–3 ✉ St.-Jacobsstraat 36 ☎ 050 34 34 65 🚌 All city buses

STADSSCHOUWBURG
www.ccbrugge.be
A renovated performance hall staging drama and music.
🔒 b2–3 ✉ Vlamingstraat 29 ☎ 050 44 30 60 🚌 4, 14, 43

LE TRAPPISTE
www.letrappiste.com
Friendly and beer-savvy staff add to the welcoming atmosphere of this vaulted cellar bar with some of the strongest brews you're likely to taste.
🔒 b2 ✉ Kuipersstraat 33 🎭 Tue–Fri 5pm–1am, Sat 5pm–2am, Sun 5pm–midnight 🚌 2, 3, 4, 5

DE WERF
www.dewerf.be
Well-established avant-garde venue that often stages live concerts of experimental jazz.
🔒 b1–2 ✉ Werfstraat 108 ☎ 050 33 05 29 🚌 41, 42

GAY BRUGES
Bruges is a gay-friendly city with a number of mixed bars and clubs. Specific venues include the easygoing@ The Pub (✉ Hallestraat 4 ☎ 0477 26 07 40) with a great stock of beers. There is also the men-only Studs Club (✉ Hoogste van Brugge 1 ☎ 476 95 31 21 🎭 Thu–Sat 10pm, Sun 3pm).

Restauants

PRICES

Prices are approximate, based on a 3-course meal for one person.

€€€ over €45
€€ €20–€45
€ under €20

BREYDEL DE CONINC (€€)

restaurant-breydel.be
Locals claim this restaurant serves the best *moules-frites* in town as well as other fish dishes, including bouillabaisse, eel Provençale and lobster with garlic butter.
➕ c3 ✉ Breidelstraat 24
☎ 050 33 97 46 🕐 Thu–Tue lunch, dinner 🚍 All buses to Markt

'T BRUGS BEERTJE (€)

www.brugsbeertje.be
The place for true beer lovers, with 300 traditionally brewed Belgian beers—many of them rare and for sale only here, and all served in their special glass. The atmosphere is as Belgian as can be. Meals are not served, but you can order snacks and cheese to enhance the beer tasting.
➕ b3 ✉ Kemelstraat 5
☎ 050 33 96 16 🕐 Mon, Thu, Fri 4pm–midnight, Sat, Sun 4pm–1am 🚍 All buses

CAFEDRAAL (€€)

www.cafedraal.be
This hidden seafood restaurant serves *waterzooi* and an excellent North Sea

bouillabaisse, in a splendid setting. There is a torchlit garden terrace.
➕ b3 ✉ Zilverstraat 38
☎ 050 34 08 45 🕐 Tue–Sat lunch, dinner 🚍 All city buses

CAFÉ VLISSINGHE (€)

www.cafevlissinghe.be
Reputedly the oldest café in Bruges, built around 1515, this is popular with locals as well as visitors. Relaxed and easygoing.
➕ c2 ✉ Blekerstraat 2
☎ 050 34 37 37 🕐 Wed–Sat 11am–midnight or later, Sun 11am–7pm 🚍 4, 14

CHEZ OLIVIER (€€)

This homey place is in an old house with fine views over one of Bruges' prettiest canals. The French fare is simple but stylish.
➕ c3 ✉ Meestraat 9 ☎ 050 33 36 59 🕐 Mon–Wed, Fri, Sat lunch, dinner 🚍 1

CHRISTOPHE (€€)

www.christophe-brugge.be
Belgians eat pretty early, but if you are looking for a place to eat after a film or concert then this is the right address. Christophe is a great bistro serving Belgian and French

BEER IN BRUGES

In the heart of town. Brouwerij De Halve Maan (✉ Walplein 26 ☎ 050 33 26 97) brews Straffe Hendrik, a wheat beer with a sweet aroma that's good with a slice of lemon.

dishes with flair. It's popular so call ahead.
➕ c3 ✉ Garenmarkt 34
☎ 050 34 48 92 🕐 Thu–Mon 7pm–2am 🚍 1, 11

DEN DYVER (€€)

www.dyver.be
Dishes here are inventive and prepared with Belgian beer. The style is old Flemish, and the view from the terrace is tops.
➕ b3 ✉ Dijver 5 ☎ 050 33 60 69 🕐 Tue–Sat lunch, dinner 🚍 1, 6, 11, 16

L'ESTAMINET (€)

Intimate café with a good snack menu. The spaghetti Bolognese is legendary. A busy summer terrace overlooks Astrid Park.
➕ c3 ✉ Park 5 ☎ 050 33 09 16 🕐 Tue, Wed, Fri–Sun 11.30am until late, Thu from 4pm 🚍 All buses to Markt

EST WIJNBAR (€)

www.wijnbarest.be
This rustic wine bar serves snacks to go with the excellent wine, including a cheese platter and a raclette, accompanied by often live jazz or blues music. The garden at the back is open in summer.
➕ c3 ✉ Braambergstraat 7
☎ 050 33 38 39 🕐 Mon, Thu, Sun 4pm–midnight, Fri, Sat 4pm–1am 🚍 All buses to Markt

DE FLORENTIJNEN (€€€)

www.deflorentijnen.be
In a much-restored house built in 1430 that origi-

nally housed the wealthy Florentine merchant community in Bruges, this restaurant continues in a classy vein but with a light contemporary touch to both the decor and the continental cuisine.

🔢 b2 ✉ Academiestraat 1 ☎ 050 67 75 33 🕐 Tue–Sat lunch, dinner 🚌 4, 14, 43

DEN GOUDEN HARYNCK (€€–€€€)

www.goudenharynck.be
The fine chef here prepares the freshest ingredients without too many frills. Dishes include pleasant surprises like smoked lobster with fig chutney and scallops with goose liver.

🔢 b–c3 ✉ Groeninge 25 ☎ 050 33 76 37 🕐 Tue–Fri lunch, dinner, Sat dinner 🚌 1

HEER HALEWIJN (€€)

Old-fashioned and well-known locally, this wine bar with brick walls and lots of candles has an excellent wine list, as well as grills on the open fire and French cheeses.

🔢 b4 ✉ Walplein 10 ☎ 050 33 92 61 🕐 Wed–Sun 6.30–10pm 🚌 1

JAN VAN EYCK (€€)

www.restauranthantvaneyck.be
Start the day with a hearty breakfast, enjoy mussels for lunch, sample home-made pancakes in the afternoon and relish pan-fried salmon or a range of delicious steaks for dinner.

🔢 c2 ✉ Jan van Eyckplein 12 ☎ 050 67 74 17 🕐 Mon,

Tue, Thu–Sat 9–5, Fri–Sat 6–9.15 🚌 4, 14, 43

DE KARMELIET (€€€)

www.dekarmeliet.be
Often regarded as Bruges' best restaurant, De Karmeliet serves the inspired Belgian cuisine of Geert Van Hecke in a stylish mansion with outside terrace.

🔢 c3 ✉ Langestraat 19 ☎ 050 33 82 59 🕐 Tue–Sat 12–1.30, 7–9.30 🚌 6

LOTUS (€€)

Originally an organic vegetarian restaurant, now it serves organic meats, too.

🔢 c3 ✉ Wapenmakersstraat 5 ☎ 050 33 10 78 🕐 Mon–Fri 11.45am–2pm 🚌 All buses to Markt

DE REPUBLIEK (€–€€)

www.derepubliek.be
Large and popular bar with high ceilings, a

BRUGGE ANNO 1468

Celebrate the wedding anniversary (3 July 1468) of Charles the Bold and Margaret of York with a gigantic four-course dinner. Beer and wine flow, and minstrels, knights, dancers and fire-eaters entertain. Reservations esssential.

✉ Vlamingstraat 86, 8000 Bruges ☎ 050 34 75 72; www.celebrations-entertainment.be 🕐 Apr–Oct Fri, Sat 7.30pm; Nov–Mar Sat 7.30pm.

---

garden in summer and a good selection of beers and international dishes.

🔢 b3 ✉ St.-Jakobsstraat 36 ☎ 050 34 02 29 🕐 Daily 11am–1am or later 🚌 All city buses

ROCK FORT (€€)

www.rock-fort.be
Trendy restaurant offering well-prepared Mediterranean dishes with a bit of Belgian and fusion. Attentive service.

🔢 c3 ✉ Langestraat 15 ☎ 050 33 41 13 🕐 Mon–Fri 12–2.30, 6.30–11 🚌 All city buses

RYAD (€€–€€€)

This excellent Moroccan restaurant is run by the charming Moroccan Mouna and her Flemish husband Philippe. Mouna serves Moroccan food as her mother prepared it for her in Fez, all fresh ingredients and cooked on the spot. Upstairs is a tearoom where you can enjoy Moroccan pastries with mint tea.

🔢 c3 ✉ Hoogstraat 32 ☎ 050 33 13 55 🕐 Daily 12–3, 6–12 🚌 All buses to Markt

TANUKI (€€)

www.tanuki.be
Classic Japanese dishes in an authentic setting with plenty of wood, a rock-tiled floor and a bamboo garden. Excellent sushi and tempura.

🔢 c4 ✉ Oude Gentweg 1 ☎ 050 34 75 12 🕐 Wed–Sun lunch, dinner 🚋 1, 11

Belgium is not a large country and many of its attractions are just a short train ride from Brussels or Bruges. Marvel at more medieval cities, cycle in the endlessly flat countryside or learn about former battles.

Sights	**96–102**	Top 25	**TOP 25**
Excursions	**103–106**	Damme ▷ **96**	
		Heysel ▷ **98**	
		Jardin Botanique Meise ▷ **100**	

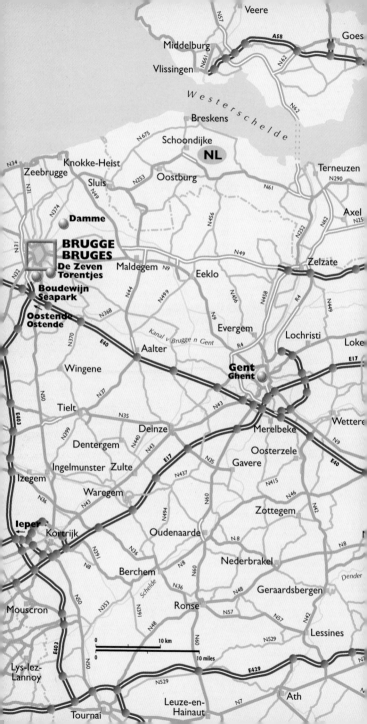

Damme

- View from the church tower
- Wooden statues of apostles
- A bicycle ride in the surrounding countryside
- A waffle or pancake in a tearoom
- Browsing the bookstores

- QuasiMundo (☎ 050 33 07 75; www.quasimundo. com) runs cycle tours from Bruges to Damme.
- Damme has declared itself a book town; you'll find books in French, Flemish and English.

When the port of Bruges dried up in the 12th century, the Bruges-Damme canal was dug and Damme became the city's new port. Sea ships went up to Damme and unloaded the goods on smaller ships to go to Bruges via the canal. The town flourished for the next hundred years.

Missing church Damme's most famous monument, the Onze-Lieve-Vrouwekerk, was built on a grand scale in 1225, but in the 18th century the upkeep costs were considered too enormous, so the part between the church tower and the still-existing part of the church was destroyed, except for the supporting arches—hence the strange shape of the church today. The interior reveals many treasures, including 13th-century wooden sculptures of the apostles and a cross found by

Modern sculpture meets historic architecture (left); sunrise over the waters (below)

fishermen from Damme in the sea, outed every year at the Holy Blood procession (▷ 83). The tower gives views over the star-shaped ramparts of the city and the surrounding countryside.

Town hall The elegant Gothic Stadhuis of 1464 has two punishment stones on the corner and some fine moldings inside the Council Hall and the Hall of Justice. In front of it, on the main square, is the 19th-century statue of the Flemish poet Jacob van Maerlant.

Food Many visitors come to Damme for lunch or dinner after a stroll or a bike ride. The many restaurants offer local fare such as Damme tart with apples, Damme sausages, *paling in 't groen* (river eel in a green sorrel sauce) and a semi-hard Damme cheese.

THE BASICS

Distance: 6.5km (4 miles) from Bruges
Journey Time: Bus 15 min
🚌 43 from Bruges' Markt
🚢 The *Lamme Goedzak* paddle steamer runs from Bruges' Noorweegse Kaai to Damme (2-hour excursion) from Apr–Sep, at 10, 12, 2, 4 and 6 (☎ 050 28 86 10)
🛈 Huyse de Grote Sterre, Jacob van Maerlantstraat 3 (www.toerismedamme.be)

Heysel

To celebrate Belgium's 100th birthday in 1930, the Centenary Stadium and Palais du Centenaire were built here. But Heysel's most famous landmark is the glitzy Atomium, a pavilion from the World Exhibition of 1958.

The Atomium The Atomium was designed in steel for Expo '58 by André Waterkeyn. Its nine balls represent the atoms of an iron crystal enlarged 165 billion times. The monument (102m/335ft high) remains an extraordinary sight, symbolizing the optimism of its time. It was built to last a year, but it became a Brussels landmark and a symbol for Belgium. At the top is a trendy Belgian restaurant with spectacular views. The ball in the middle has a bar, several other balls are used for temporary exhibitions and one, Kids

The Atomium has become a symbol of Brussels

World, is dedicated to children. In a nearby pavilion is Salon '58, a trendy restaurant-bar, decorated in 1950s style and offering views of the Atomium.

Permanent exhibition *Atomium. From Symbol to Icon* tells the history of the pavilion and the events of Expo '58. Special exhibitions on the themes of Science, Progress and the Future are staged at the Atomium and have covered such diverse subjects as progressive architecture, modern design and environmental projects. The Atomium shop has a wide range of books, DVDs and gifts.

Trade space The Stade Roi Baudouin hosts sports events and rock concerts, while the Palais du Centenaire forms the core of the Trade Mart, with 10 exhibition halls.

FARTHER AFIELD TOP 25

THE BASICS

Distance: 2.4km (1.5 miles) from the heart of Brussels
Journey Time: 25 min

Atomium
www.atomium.be
✉ Blvd du Centenaire
☎ 02 475 4775
🕐 Daily 10–6
💰 Expensive
Ⓜ Heysel/Heizel
♿ Few

Jardin Botanique Meise

TOP
25

- The fabulous 13 glass-houses of the Plant Palace
- Garden walks
- The Orangery restaurant

TIP

- Take a stroll among oak and conifer trees, magnolias, rhododendrons and wild roses in the northwest section of the garden.

The Jardin Botanique Meise (formerly known as the National Botanic Garden of Belgium) is one of the largest botanical gardens in the world. It has more than 18,000 types of plants, a herbarium of 3 million species and a library of 70,000 botanical works and journals, all housed within 92ha (227 acres) of the grounds of the old Castle Bouchout at Meise.

Plant Palace The Botanical Garden dates from the early 19th century when Belgium was in the control of the Dutch. Until 1958, the garden was located in the middle of Brussels on a site that is now the Botanical Garden of Brussels. Today's garden has an extensive complex of greenhouses, including the huge Plant Palace where individual greenhouses contain

Clockwise from top left: inside the greenhouse of the Plant Palace; studying a giant fern; giant water lilies; the gardens lie in the grounds of Castle Bouchout

fascinating specimens from areas such as the Mediterranean and the tropical rain forest. In the Evolution House you can trace the development of plants over the past 500 million years.

Conservation The range of species is outstanding and includes bamboos, fuchsias, orchids, hydrangeas and camellias. The Herbarium displays a summer spread of herbaceous perennials while there is even a garden full of plants used in traditional medicine. The Botanic Garden's extensive research programs have earned it an international reputation in the field of plant conservation and tropical and European plant study. The garden also has a restaurant—the Orangery—and a garden shop with an excellent array of plant books, postcards and floral calendars. You can also buy seeds, honey, preserves and even botanical jewelry.

THE BASICS

www.br.fgov.be
Distance: 12km
(7.5 miles) from the heart
of Brussels
Journey Time: 1 hour
✉ Nieuwelaan 38, 1860
Meise
☎ 02 260 0970
🕐 Mid-Mar to mid-Oct
daily 9.30–5.30; mid-Oct to
mid-Mar 9.30–4.30
🚌 De Lijn bus 250, 251
from Brussels
♿ Good
🍴 Orangery restaurant
(🕐 Mar–Nov daily 11–6)
✋ Moderate

More to See

BASILIQUE NATIONALE DU SACRÉ-COEUR

The basilica's massive green dome is one of Brussels' landmarks, but inside is gloomy. Built between 1905 and 1979, the world's sixth-largest church was meant to symbolize unity between Belgium's Flemish and French-speaking communities. The views from the dome are superb.

🏠 A1 ✉ Parvis de la Basilique 1 ☎ 02 421 1660 🕐 Daily 10–6 (until 5 in winter). Dome Mar–Oct Mon–Fri 9–5; Nov–Feb 10–4 🚇 Simonis, then tram 19 💷 Free; entry to the dome inexpensive

BOUDEWIJN SEAPARK

www.boudewijnseapark.be

A great amusement park for both younger kids and teenagers, with Europe's most sophisticated dolphinarium.

🏠 South of Bruges ✉ A. De Baeckestraat 12, St.-Michiels ☎ 050 38 38 38 🕐 Apr daily 11–5; May, Jun daily 10.30–5; Jul, Aug daily 10–6. At other times of the year call ahead to check the park is open 🚌 7, 17 from railway station 🦽 Good 💷 Expensive

BRUPARCK

www.minieurope.com

Bruparck hosts Mini-Europe, with 300 miniature models of monuments in the EU. There is also a water funpark, Océade, and cinemas, Kinepolis.

🏠 North of Brussels ✉ Boulevard du Centenaire 20, Heysel ☎ 02 478 0550 🕐 Varies 🚇 Heysel/Heizel 🦽 Good 💷 Expensive

LAEKEN

Laeken is home to the royal family, whose palace, the Château Royal, is closed to the public. The exquisite Serres Royales (Royal Greenhouses), with an amazing variety of tropical plants, are open during April and May. Nearby is the pretty Parc de Laeken.

🏠 North of Brussels ✉ Boulevard de Smet de Naeyer 🚇 Stuyvenberg 🚋 Tram 23, 51

DE ZEVEN TORENTJES

This former 14th-century farm estate is now a children's farm.

🏠 Southeast of Bruges ✉ Canadaring 41, Assebroek ☎ 050 35 40 43 🕐 Mon–Fri 8.30–12, 2–4 🚌 2

Flowerbeds in front of the Basilique Nationale du Sacré-Coeur

A view of Brussels' spires and sky-scrapers from the Parc de Laeken

Excursions

ANTWERP

Antwerp is a lively Flemish city, famous for Belgian fashion. The ModeMuseum (MoMu) has a historic costume and lace collection, and organizes major fashion exhibitions. Many Belgian designers have a shop in the city.

Not just fashion Antwerp is also the city of Rubens, whose work can be seen at his house, the Rubenshuis, and at the wonderful Koninklijk Museum voor Schone Kunsten (Fine Arts Museum), which has a large collection of Flemish Primitives and works from Antwerp's Golden Age (17th century). MUHKA (Museum for Contemporary Art) features temporary exhibitions. The heart of Antwerp is the Grote Markt square and the Onze-Lieve-Vrouwe Cathedral, the largest Gothic church in Belgium. The main shopping street is the elegant Meir.

THE BASICS

www.visitantwerpen.be
Distance: 45km (27 miles) from Brussels; 105km (65 miles) from Bruges
Journey Time: 40 min (Brussels); 1 hour (Bruges)
🚆 Several trains an hour from Brussels and Bruges
🛈 Grote Markt 13 (tel 03 232 0103)

Below from left to right: guildhouses on Antwerp's Grote Markt; reflections of waterside buildings on Korenlei, Ghent; mosaics in the Zurenborg district of Antwerp, an architectural conservation area

GHENT

Ghent is pretty much undiscovered compared to Bruges and Brussels, but it's a lively city full of Flemish architecture and art. With a large university, there is a young vibe and vibrant nightlife.

Medieval treasures At the heart of the city is the Gravensteen, the impressive 12th-century medieval castle of the Counts of Flanders. A short walk away is the 14th-century Sint-Baafskathedraal, which hides the city's greatest treasure, Jan van Eyck's *Adoration of the Mystic Lamb*. Across from the cathedral is the Lakenhalle, the 15th-century Cloth Hall, and the majestic Belfort (belfry tower), with great views over the city. On Graslei and Korenlei are several guildhouses.

THE BASICS

www.visitgent.be
Distance: 56km (35 miles) from Brussels; 42km (26 miles) from Bruges
Journey Time: 40 min (Brussels); 30 min (Bruges)
🚆 Several trains each hour from Bruges and Brussels
🛈 Sint-Veerleplein 5 (tel 09 266 5660)
🍽 Some of the city's best restaurants are in the narrow alleys of Patershol

FARTHER AFIELD EXCURSIONS

IEPER AND WAR MEMORIALS

During the 12th century Ieper (Ypres) was an important cloth trade hub, together with Ghent and Bruges.

Historic city Many of Ieper's important monuments date from that time, including the Lakenhalle (Cloth Hall), with 48 doors giving access to the spacious halls, the adjacent Belfry (70m/230ft high) and the Gothic Sint-Maartens-kathedraal. During World War I, the city was bombarded for four years and reduced to ruins, while 500,000 soldiers died in the "Ypres Salient." The rebuilding of the city took more than 40 years and 170 war cemeteries in the area pay tribute to the fallen soldiers. The In Flanders Field Museum tells Ypres' story during World War I.

THE BASICS

www.toerisme-ieper.be
www.greatwar.be
Distance: 100km
(62 miles) from Brussels;
50km (31 miles) from
Bruges
🚆 Several direct trains
each day from Brussels
(1.5 hours) or via Kortrijk (2
hours); from Bruges change
trains in Kortrijk (1.5 hours)
ℹ️ Lakenhalle, Grote Markt
(tel 057 23 92 20)

OSTEND

This lively town is popular with Belgians, who come for a walk on the long beach on weekends, to eat in one of the many fish restaurants around the port or to spend the evening in one of the bars.

Royal connections The royal family chose Ostend for their summer residence, which earned it the name "Queen of Belgian Beach Resorts." Now, the Royal Villa built by Léopold I has long been sold and has become a museum. Art lovers should pay a visit to the Museum voor Schone Kunsten (Museum of Fine Arts), which has works by James Ensor and Flemish painters Permeke and Spilliaert. You can wander around Ensor's former house and studio, now called the James Ensor House. The interesting P.M.M.K. (Museum of Modern Art) in an old warehouse, illustrates Belgian modern art.

THE BASICS

www.visitoostende.be
Distance: 100km
(62 miles) from Brussels;
30km (19 miles) from
Bruges
🚆 Direct train from
Brussels (1.5 hours); from
Bruges (20 min)
ℹ️ Monacoplein 2
(tel 059 70 11 99)

Ghent (left) is a vibrant city, full of Flemish architecture. Ostend (below) is one of Belgium's largest resorts

THE BASICS

www.walibi.be
Distance: 16km (10 miles) from Brussels
Journey Time: 25 min
✉ E411 Brussels-Namur, exit 6, in Wavres ☎ 010 42 15 00 🕐 Phone or check website for opening times 🚉 Train from Gare Schuman to Gare de Bierges on Ottignies/Louvain-la-Neuve line (short walk from station) ♿ Few
✋ Very expensive

WALIBI

Walibi, formerly known as Six Flags Belgium, is a spectacular theme park near Brussels, with a wide range of rides and attractions for all ages.

Feeling brave? Rides include the Werewolf, at 32m (105ft) the highest wooden roller coaster in Belgium, which hurtles you along 1,000m (1,090 yards) of track at an average speed of 80km/h (50mph). Another exhilarating ride is the Cobra, which propels riders at 75km/h (46mph) into a series of double spirals and through hair-raising loops. Smaller kids have their own area of more gentle rides and can play together with Bugs Bunny and his pals.

THE BASICS

www.waterloo1815.be
Distance: 20km (12.5 miles) from Brussels
Journey Time: 20 mins
🚉 From Gare du Midi, Centrale, Nord. Waterloo station is 1km (0.6 miles) from the heart of Waterloo; you can rent bicycles at Braine-l'Alleud station
ℹ Route du Lion 315, Braine-l'Alleud (tel 02 385 1912)
Musée Wellington
☎ 02 357 2860
Napoleon's Last HQ
☎ 02 384 2424
Visitor Center
☎ 02 385 1912

WATERLOO

Here is the famous battlefield where the Duke of Wellington defeated Napoleon Bonaparte on 18 June 1815, ending France's military domination of Europe.

Looking back Most people come to see the Butte du Lion (pictured above and below right), a grass-covered pyramid built by local women with soil from the battlefield to mark the spot where William of Orange, one of Wellington's commanders and later King of the Netherlands, was wounded. Climb the 226 steps for the views. At the foot of the mound is the Visitor Center, with the Waterloo Panorama. The Musée Wellington, in the inn where the Duke lodged, shows battle memorabilia. So does le Caillou, a farm where Napoleon had his last headquarters. A motorway now cuts through the battlefield, but for a clearer idea of what happened, attend the reenactment (every five years in June, next due in 2015).

Whatever your tastes and budget, there's plenty of choice for places to stay in Brussels and Bruges. If you haven't already booked your hotel, it's worth checking out the Internet to catch some deals.

Introduction   108

Budget Hotels   109

Mid-Range Hotels   110–111

Luxury Hotels   112

Where to Stay

Introduction

Brussels and Bruges have a large choice of accommodations, from the most luxurious to the most simple. Standards are usually fairly high, but some hotels, in Brussels in particular, lack beauty or special character. Most places include breakfast in the overnight rate, but if it is not included, count on paying €5–€15 extra.

Brussels

As the European capital, Brussels has no shortage of hotels, but many of these are geared toward businesspeople. This means that there are a large number of the smarter chain hotels such as the Hilton, Sheraton, Marriott, Hyatt, Conrad and Novotel. These hotels, and in fact most hotels in town, often offer bargain rates on weekends and during the summer, when the bureaucrats leave town. All year round, but particularly in the spring and fall, it pays to reserve ahead, as the city fills up quickly. Belgium's central reservation agency, Resotel (tel 02 779 3939; www.belgium-hospitality.com), will reserve rooms for you and check for special offers and discounts. For the impulsive, the Brussels International tourist office, on the Grand' Place, operates a free same-night booking service.

Bruges

There is less need to reserve ahead in Bruges outside the summer months and weekends, but it is safer to do so. Bruges has some very romantic hotels on the canals, which are included in our listings.

BED-AND-BREAKFAST

As an alternative to hotel accommodations, both Brussels and Bruges have an increasing number of charming bed-and-breakfasts. These are usually good quality and less expensive than hotels, and you get the chance to ask the owners for inside information on the best places to visit. Tourist offices can arrange B&B rooms or you can check the list of B&Bs on their website. In Brussels, Bed & Brussels (www.bnb-brussels.be) has an online booking service, as has Taxistop (www.taxistop.be).

Budget Hotels

PRICES

Expect to pay under €90 per night for a double room in a budget hotel.

BRUSSELS

A LA GRANDE CLOCHE

www.hotelgrandecloche.com
There are good-size rooms in this hotel, on a quiet square near the happening St.-Géry area and Grand' Place. The service is relaxed but very friendly.
➕ D6 ✉ Place Rouppe 10 ☎ 02 512 6140 Ⓖ Gare du Midi/Anneessens

LES BLUETS

www.bluets.be
This small and friendly hotel is in a grand 19th-century building. The 10 rooms are decorated with old objets d'art, paintings and mirrors. Smoking is not allowed.
➕ E8 ✉ Rue Berckmans 124 ☎ 02 534 3983 Ⓖ Hôtel des Monnaies

HÔTEL GALIA

www.hotelgalia.com
A modernized hotel, the Galia overlooks the flea market of the Marolles, while the surrounding area has all the street style of authentic Brussels. The rooms, decorated with comic strips, are clean and comfortable.
➕ D7 ✉ Place du Jeu de Balle 15–16 ☎ 02 502 42 43 Ⓖ Porte de Hal/Halleitoort

LA LÉGENDE

www.hotellalegende.com
Attractive and very good-value hotel, with 26 rooms around an internal courtyard. It is ideally located near Manneken Pis and the Grand' Place, as well as the bars and restaurants of St.-Géry.
➕ D–E5 ✉ Rue du Lombard 35 ☎ 02 512 8290 🚋 Tram 23, 55, 56, 81

PHILEAS FOGG

www.phileasfoggbrussels.com
Beautiful, welcoming bed-and-breakfast with four rooms, furnished with antiques, Belgian art and objects picked up by the owner on her travels. Also three studio flats. It's a gay-friendly establishment.
➕ G4 ✉ Rue van Bemmel 65 ☎ 32 495 22 09 85 Ⓖ Madou/Botanique 🚋 Tram 92, 93

INEXPENSIVE HOTELS

Many hotels in Brussels are business-oriented, so in summer and on weekends prices can drop by up to 50 percent. The Belgian Tourist Reservations office on Grand' Place (☎ 02 513 7484) has a free list of more than 800 hotels offering off-peak reductions. Although this makes it difficult to reserve far in advance, hotels are less full in these periods. Alternatively, you could try bed-and-breakfast accommodations (▷ 108).

SLEEP WELL

www.sleepwell.be
This former YMCA has good rooms and dormitory beds at hostel rates. There is no longer a lock-out, and the central location is excellent.
➕ E4 ✉ Rue du Damier 23 ☎ 02 218 5050 Ⓖ Rogier/De Brouckère 🚋 Tram 92, 93

BRUGES

BAUHAUS

www.bauhaus.be
Popular central hostel with free sheets and showers. Part of it is now a one-star hotel, with rooms that have a private shower. There is a very popular bar downstairs.
➕ d3 ✉ Langestraat 127–133 ☎ 050 34 10 93 🚌 6, 16

B&B MARIE-PAULE GESQUIÈRE

Three comfortable rooms in an ivy-clad house overlooking a park by the city walls and windmills. Very good breakfast with eggs and Belgian chocolate.
➕ d2 ✉ Oostproosse 14 ☎ 050 33 92 46 🚌 4, 16

HOTEL BLA BLA

www.hotelblabla.com
The former Imperial hotel has been renovated and renamed Bla Bla. It makes an ideal Bruges city base.
➕ b3 ✉ 24–28 Dweersstraat ☎ 050 33 90 14 🚌 All buses to 't Zand

Mid-Range Hotels

BRUSSELS

LE 9 HOTEL CENTRAL
www.le9hotel.com
This cool and comfy hotel boasts chic design interiors behind its classical Brussels facade. Exposed brickwork and attractive wooden artifacts in the rooms set the tone for the modernist style.
🚩 E5 ✉ Koloniënstraat 10 ☎ 02 504 9910 🚇 Gare Centrale 🚊 Tram 92, 93

ARLEQUIN
www.florishotels.com
A three-star hotel close to the Grand' Place, with 92 comfortable rooms. A buffet breakfast is served in the 7th Heaven dining room, which has views of the Grand' Place.
🚩 E5 ✉ Rue de la Fourche 17–19 ☎ 02 514 1615 🚇 Bourse/Gare Centrale

ATLAS HOTEL
www.atlas-hotel.be
The Atlas has been modernized. It has smartly furnished rooms and is in a quiet location, but within walking distance of the buzzing heart of the city.
🚩 D5 ✉ Rue du Vieux Marché aux Grains 30 ☎ 02 502 6006 🚇 Bourse/Beurs 🚊 89, 127, 128

EXE SABLON
www.exesablonhotel.com
A modern, efficient hotel, with 32 rooms.
🚩 E6 ✉ Rue de la Paille 2–8, Sablon ☎ 02 513 6040 🚊 Tram 92, 93

HOTEL-CAFÉ PACIFIC
www.hotelcafepacific.com
A stylish small hotel with bright art deco ambience and a similarly stylish lounge bar.
🚩 D5 ✉ Rue Antoine Dansaert 57 ☎ 02 213 0080 🚇 Bourse/Beurs 🚊 89, 126, 127

METROPOLE
www.metropolehotel.com
This grand hotel, opened in 1895, has wonderful architecture in the public spaces. The bedrooms are more simple but comfortable, and weekend rates are good value.
🚩 E4 ✉ Place de Brouckère 31 ☎ 02 217 2300 🚇 De Brouckère 🚊 Tram 3, 4, 31, 32

GRAND MIROIR

One of Brussels' oldest hotels was the Hôtel du Grand Miroir, at 26 rue de la Montagne. It was run by a Parisian, and its most famous resident was French poet Charles Baudelaire (1821–67), who came to live here to escape his creditors in Paris. Toward the end of his life he wrote a travel book called *Pauvre Belgique!* in which he condemned the whole nation and especially Brussels, its men, women, children, streets, food, customs, journalism and politics. The beautiful hotel was destroyed in 1956.

MONTY
www.monty-hotel.be
Far from the heart of town but convenient for the EU Quarter and Le Cinquantenaire, this small boutique hotel has 18 spacious rooms, meticulously designed in a modernist warm style. The rooms are furnished with designs by Philippe Starck, Charles Eames, A. Castiglioni and Ingo Maurer, among others, and the atmosphere is elegant. Friendly service.
🚩 Off map J6 ✉ Boulevard Brand Whitlock 101 ☎ 02 734 5636 🚇 Georges-Henri

MOZART
www.hotel-mozart.be
In a lovely 17th-century building right in the heart of Brussels, the hotel has 50 rooms decorated in opulent Louis XV style.
🚩 E5 ✉ Rue Marché aux Fromages 23 ☎ 02 502 6661 🚇 Bourse/Gare Centrale

NOGA
www.nogahotel.com
Tranquil, charming hotel located in the Ste.-Catherine district, near the hip hangouts on the rue Dansaert and rue des Flandres.
🚩 D4 ✉ Rue du Béguinage 38 ☎ 02 218 6763 🚇 Ste.-Catherine/St.-Katelijne

ST.-MICHEL

www.hotelsaintmichel.be
Family-run, 15-room hotel
behind the gilded facade
of the House of the Duke
of Brabant. Grand' Place
can be noisy at night.
⊕ E5 ✉ Grand' Place 15 ☎ 02
511 0956 🚇 Gare Centrale/
Bourse 🚊 Tram 3, 4, 31, 32

WELCOME

www.hotelwelcome.com
Family-run hotel on a
quiet street near the fash-
ionable area around rue
Dansaert. The 15 rooms
are decorated in the style
of other countries.
⊕ D4 ✉ Quai au Bois à
Brûler 23 ☎ 02 219 9546
🚇 Ste.-Catherine/St.-Katelijne

🔲 **BRUGES**

ADORNES

www.adornes.be
Quiet three-star hotel in
a beautiful old Flemish
house overlooking a
canal. The rooms are
comfortable, and break-
fast is served in a lovely
room with a fireplace.
Friendly service.
⊕ c2 ✉ St.-Annarei 26
☎ 050 34 13 36 🕐 Closed
Jan to 1st weekend in Feb
🚌 4, 14

ANSELMUS

www.anselmus.be
Pleasant hotel in a
17th-century mansion
in a quiet street. The
spacious rooms are
stylishly decorated, and
breakfast is good, too.
⊕ c2–3 ✉ Ridderstraat 15
☎ 050 34 13 74 🕐 Closed

Jan to mid-Feb and 1st two
weeks in Jul 🚌 All buses
to Markt

DE GOEZEPUT

www.hotelgoezeput.be
Delightful small hotel in
an 18th-century mon-
astery. The rooms ooze
charm and the cellar-bar
is popular with locals.
⊕ b3 ✉ Goezeputstraat 29
☎ 050 34 26 94 🚌 All buses
to t'Zand

GRAND HOTEL
DU SABLON

www.hotelsablon.be
Traditional hotel with
stained-glass art nouveau
dome and 36 rooms,
offering modern facilities.
The rear of the hotel was
an inn 400 years ago.

🔲 **PARKING IN BRUGES**

The use of a parking disc
is compulsory to park in
the heart of Bruges from
Monday to Saturday (except
public holidays) 9am–7pm,
and parking is allowed for up
to four hours. Several streets
have been reserved for resi-
dents' parking. Visitors are
encouraged to drop off their
luggage at their hotel and
then park the car in one of
the large car parks in the city
(€8.70/24 hours) or the
P Centrum car park near
the train station (€2.50/24
hours), with a free bus service to the heart of the city.
Central Bruges is quite small
and most of the sights are
easily reached on foot.

⊕ b3 ✉ Kopstraat 10 ☎ 02
473 63 97 52 🚌 All buses
to Mark

HUYZE DIE MAENE

www.huyzediemaene.be
This bed-and-breakfast
has just two luxurious
rooms and a sumptuous
suite but the location
is as central as it gets.
Reserve in advance as
this is a popular spot.
⊕ b3 ✉ Markt 17
☎ 050 33 39 59 🚌 All buses
to Markt

HOTEL MONTANUS

www.montanus.be
Romantic family-run
boutique hotel in a 17th-
century mansion with an
interior garden. 20 chic
rooms with a luxury feel.
⊕ c3 ✉ Nieuwe Gentweg 78
☎ 050 33 11 76 🚌 1, 11

PRINSENHOF

www.prinsenhof.be
Quiet and sumptuous
16-room hotel decorated
in elegant Burgundian
style with chandeliers,
antiques, four-poster beds
and moulded ceilings.
⊕ b3 ✉ Ontvangersstraat 9
☎ 050 34 26 90 🚌 All buses
to Markt

RELAIS OUD HUIS
AMSTERDAM

www.oha.be
Attractive renovation of
two 17th-century houses,
furnished with antiques
and overlooking a canal.
The 34 rooms are
individually decorated.
⊕ c2 ✉ Genthof 4a
☎ 050 34 18 10 🚌 4, 14

Luxury Hotels

PRICES

Expect to pay more than €150 per night for a double room in a luxury hotel.

BRUSSELS

AMIGO
www.hotelamigo.com
One of Brussels' finest hotels (▷ panel), the Amigo is in the style of an 18th-century mansion. The staff are friendly and the 176 rooms are elegantly furnished. It is popular with ministers and French media stars.
✚ E5 ✉ Rue de l'Amigo 1–3 ☎ 02 547 4747
🚇 Bourse/Beurs, Gare Centrale

LE DIXSEPTIÈME
www.ledixseptieme.be
Stylish hotel in the 17th-century former residence of the Spanish ambassador, located between the Grand' Place and Central Station. The 24 elegant rooms are arranged around a tranquil courtyard.
✚ E5 ✉ Rue de la Madeleine 25 ☎ 02 517 1717 🚇 Gare Centrale/Centraal Station

MARRIOTT BRUSSELS
www.marriott.com
Good value five-star hotel with spacious rooms and excellent service, right in the heart of the city, near the shopping and nightlife areas of St.-Géry and Ste.-Catherine and a five-minute walk from the Grand' Place.
✚ D5 ✉ Rue Auguste Orts 3–7 ☎ 02 516 9090
🚇 Bourse/Beurs

STEIGENBERGER GRANDHOTEL BRUSSELS
en.steigenberger.com
One of the city's grandest hotels, with 250 stylish and sumptuous rooms, all five-star amenities, some great restaurants and perfect service. It is located at the heart of Brussels' upscale shopping district.
✚ E7–8 ✉ Avenue Louise 71 ☎ 02 542 4242 🚇 Louise

WARWICK BARSEY HOTEL BRUSSELS
www.warwickbarsey.com
This ultrachic hotel has 99 rooms and suites decorated in rich colors, with textiles and objets d'art that give a homey feeling. The restaurant, Le Barsey, attracts celebrities and artists.
✚ G10 ✉ Avenue Louise 381–383 ☎ 02 649 9800
🚌 Tram 93, 94

BRUGES

DE ORANGERIE
www.hotelorangerie.com
Nineteen tasteful rooms in a renovated 15th-century convent covered in ivy and filled with antiques and objets d'art. This romantic boutique hotel overlooks one of Bruges' prettiest corners and in summer breakfast is served by the canal.
✚ c3 ✉ Karhtuizerinnen-straat 10 ☎ 050 34 16 49
🚌 1, 6, 11, 16

ROMANTIK PANDHOTEL
www.pandhotel.com
An 18th-century carriage house hidden in a leafy square has been converted into a small and stylish hotel decorated with antiques and objets d'art. The 23 rooms are sumptuous but not over-stated.
✚ c3 ✉ Pandreitje 16
☎ 050 34 06 66
🚌 All buses

DE TUILERIEEN
www.hoteltuilerieen.com
A 16th-century mansion with 45 rooms and views of one of Bruges' most beautiful canals, the Dijver.
✚ c3 ✉ Dijver 7 ☎ 050 34 36 91 🚌 1, 6, 11, 16

AMIGO

The Amigo stands on the site of Brussels' former city prison, which, like the hotel now, had its fair share of celebrity occupants. The 19th-century French poet Paul Verlaine shot his lover Arthur Rimbaud in the wrist in the street and ended up here, and so did Karl Marx after the police found communist publications in his rooms at the Hôtel Le Bois Sauvage, on place Ste.-Gudule.

Use this section to familiarize yourself with travel to and within Brussels and Bruges. The Essential Facts will give you some insider knowledge of the cities and you'll also find some language tips.

Planning Ahead   **114–115**

Getting There   **116–117**

Getting Around   **118–119**

Essential Facts   **120–121**

Language   **122–123**

Timeline   **124–125**

Planning Ahead

When to Go

Belgium has warm summers and mild winters. The country's northern location gives it gloriously long summer nights, perfect for enjoying outdoor cafés. The peak tourist season is July and August, when the crowds add to the buzz in Brussels but can overwhelm Bruges.

> **TIME**
> Belgium is one hour ahead of GMT, 6 hours ahead of New York and 9 hours ahead of Los Angeles.

AVERAGE DAILY MAXIMUM TEMPERATURES

JAN	FEB	MAR	APR	MAY	JUN	JUL	AUG	SEP	OCT	NOV	DEC
5°C	6°C	9°C	11°C	15°C	18°C	20°C	20°C	19°C	15°C	10°C	6°C
41°F	43°F	48°F	52°F	59°F	64°F	68°F	68°F	66°F	59°F	50°F	43°F

Spring (April to May) may take a while to arrive, but by May the weather is warmer and sunnier.

Summer (June to August) can be glorious—or cloudy and rainy.

Fall (September to November) sees mild temperatures, and there can be good, clear days, especially in September and October.

Winter (December to March) has little snow and the temperatures rarely get below freezing, but it rains frequently, sometimes accompanied by strong winds and hail.

WHAT'S ON

April *Brussels International Fantastic Film Festival* (☎ 02 201 1713)
Brussels Film Festival (www.befilmfestival.be).

April–May Brussels' Royal Greenhouses (Serres Royales) open to the public (▷ 102).

May *Procession of the Holy Blood* in Bruges (▷ 83).
Brussels Jazz Marathon (www.brussels jazzmarathon. be).
Brussels Half Marathon: A run of 20km (12.5 miles).
Summer Festival (May/Jun–Sep): Classical concerts in Brussels.

June Reenactment of the Battle of Waterloo at Waterloo (mid-Jun, every five years; next event in 2015).

July *Brussels Ommegang* (first Thu).
Cactus Festival in Bruges (second weekend): open-air concerts (www.cactusfestival.be).
Foire du Midi (mid-Jul to mid-Aug): largest fair in Europe, in Brussels.
National Day (21 Jul): Festivities in Brussels.

August Raising of the *Meiboom*, or maypole, in Brussels (9 Aug).
Floral carpet (mid-Aug, even-numbered years): on Brussels' Grand' Place.
Reiefeesten or Festival of the Canals (every four years; next in 2017) in Bruges.

August–September
Praalstoet van de Gouden Boomstoet or Pageant of the Golden Tree (every five years) in Bruges; next, 2017.
Heritage Days: Hundreds of houses and monuments open to the public in Belgium.

October–December
Europalia: Arts and cultural events in Brussels.
Modo Brussels: Contemporary fashion designs by the hottest young Brussels designers are featured at various locations.

NEED TO KNOW PLANNING AHEAD

Brussels and Bruges Online

www.beercapital.be
This site is a guide to Belgian beers, with a description of the different varieties, where they are brewed and sold, walking tours and guided tours, and, of course, a list of the best bars.

www.brugge.be
A site run by the tourist office in Bruges that has practical information, virtual walks through the city, history and recommendations for hotels, restaurants and excursions.

www.bruggecitycard.be
The website for information about the Brugge City Card (48 hours €43, 72 hours €48). Contains useful information on city museums, transportation, sightseeing and cultural events.

www.visitbrussels.be/www.visitbelgium.com
The website of the Brussels tourist office has plenty of suggestions on how to discover the city over a weekend. Lots of practical information, a few quirky ideas, inexpensive hotel deals and a virtual comic-strip walk.

www.brusselsartnouveau.be
This site has plenty of information about Brussels' art nouveau buildings, which made the city one of the art nouveau capitals of Europe, along with Vienna and Barcelona.

www.noctis.com
Listings of bars, clubs, parties, music events and festivals, as well as information for gay visitors.

www.tintinologist.org
Everything you ever wanted to know about Tintin, Belgium's comic strip hero.

www.visitflanders.com
This excellent website, run by the Tourism Flanders office in Brussels, offers information on Bruges, Brussels and the rest of Flanders and also gives a bird's-eye view of the region.

GOOD TRAVEL SITES

www.fodors.com
A complete travel-planning site. You can research prices and weather; book air tickets, cars and rooms; ask questions (and get answers) from fellow visitors; and find links to other sites.

www.trabel.com
The award-winning site of Belgium Travel Network has general information about Belgium, but specializes in practical information on car rental, travel, airlines, hotels and nightlife.

INTERNET ACCESS

Hotels without WiFi are now rare in modern Brussels and Bruges. Many public spaces have Internet access and the main metro stations in Brussels, such as De Brouckère and Rogier, have Internet points or cafés. There is public Internet access throughout Bruges city center.

Getting There

INSURANCE

EU nationals receive emergency medical treatment with the European Health Insurance Card. Obtain one before visiting. Full health and travel insurance is still advised. US visitors should check their health coverage before departure. Full insurance is advised for all other visitors.

MAPS

In Brussels, street names and metro stations are marked in French and Flemish. In Bruges, street names are in Flemish only. Pick up free bus maps (and metro maps in Brussels) and timetables from tourist offices, the metro, the STIB/MIVB office in Brussels' Gare du Midi station and the bus office at Bruges rail station.

NEED TO KNOW GETTING THERE

AIRPORTS AND PORTS

Belgium's principal international airport is Zaventem, 14km (9 miles) northeast of Brussels. Eurostar trains from London arrive at Brussels' Gare du Midi station. Car ferries arrive at the ports of Zeebrugge and Oostende.

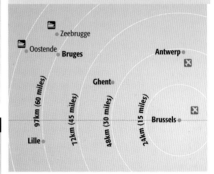

ARRIVING BY AIR

The Airport City Express shuttle train (☎ 02 528 2828; www.belgianrail.be) takes passengers from Brussels Airport (☎ 0900 70000; www.brusselsairport.be) to Brussels' main railway stations every 15–20 minutes (🕐 5.12am– midnight; journey time 16–26 minutes; cost €8.50). The Airport Line (☎ 0900 10310; www.stib.be) has three bus services to the heart of Brussels—bus No. 12; journey time 35 minutes; cost €4. De Lijn (☎ 02 526 2820; www.delijn.be) also runs buses from the airport to the Gare du Nord (🕐 6am–midnight; 45 minutes; cost €2.70).

Regular trains leave from Brussels' South, North and Central stations to Bruges (☎ 02 528 2828; www.belgianrail.be) 4.30am–11pm (journey time one hour; cost €14.10). Taxis outside the airport's arrivals hall display a blue-and-yellow

Map labels: Zeebrugge, Oostende, Bruges, Antwerp, Ghent, Brussels, Lille; 97km (60 miles), 72km (45 miles), 48km (30 miles), 24km (15 miles)

emblem, but they are expensive (around €45 to Brussels). Many accept credit cards; confirm with the driver before you travel.

ARRIVING BY BUS

Eurolines buses connect major European cities with Brussels (www.eurolines.com). The international bus station is CCN Gare du Nord/Noordstation (✉ Rue du Progrès 80 ☎ 02 274 1350). There are direct buses from London to Bruges, as well as frequent trains from the three main Brussels' stations to Bruges.

ARRIVING BY TRAIN

High-speed Eurostar trains from London arrive at Brussels' Gare du Midi (journey time 2 hours; www.eurostar.com). Trains to Bruges leave from the same station. Thalys trains from Paris and TGV trains from around France and ICE trains from Germany also arrive at Gare du Midi. Trains connect many major European cities to Brussels, and there are trains from Germany and Holland to Bruges.

ARRIVING BY SEA

P&O Ferries operates car ferries from Hull in the UK to Zeebrugge (www.poferries.com; journey time 14 hours). TransEuropa Ferries (www.transeuropaferries.com; 4 hours) operate car ferries (no foot passengers or coaches) from Ramsgate to Oostende (Ostend). There are 20 sailings a day but only eight of these cater to cars. To drive from Zeebrugge to Bruges take the N31 and N371 (15 minutes), and to Brussels the N31 and E40 (1 hour 15 minutes); from Ostend to Bruges take the A10 (15 minutes). Other companies, like SeaFrance and P&O ferries, cross from Dover to Calais in about 75 minutes. By car from Calais to Bruges take the E40 (1 hour 20 minutes); to Brussels take the E15 (2 hours). Eurotunnel takes cars from Folkestone to Coquelles, near Calais, in France in 35 minutes (UK ☎ 08443 353535; www.eurotunnel.com; 24 hours).

PASSPORTS/VISAS

Always check the latest entry requirements before you travel, as regulations can change at short notice.

VISITORS WITH DISABILITIES

There are few facilities on buses, trams and the metro for people with disabilities, but a minibus service equipped for wheelchairs is available at low cost from the public transport network STIB/MIVB (☎ 02 515 2365; www.stib.be). On trains outside Brussels, a passenger accompanying a passenger with disabilities travels free.

Few buildings in Brussels and Bruges have facilities for people with disabilities, and the streets have uneven cobblestones, which are tough on wheelchairs. For more information, contact Mobility International (✉ Boulevard Baudouin 18 📞 02 201 5608; email: mobint@dproducts.be).

NEED TO KNOW GETTING THERE

Getting Around

BICYCLING TOURS

● In Bruges several companies offer bicycle tours with a guide, around the city or to the surrounding countryside, including Damme and Oostburg. One of the best is QuasiMundo Biketours (☎ 050 33 07 75; www.quasimundo.com). Others include the Pink Bear Bike Tours (☎ 050 61 66 86; www.pinkbear. freeservers. com) and the Green Bike Tour (☎ 050 61 26 67; www.arlando.be/ greenbiketour.htm).

● In Brussels, Pro Vélo organizes interesting bicycling tours with different themes (☎ 02 502 7355; www.provelo.org).

HORSE AND CARTS

Horse and carts, or *calèches*, are a popular way to see the historical heart of Bruges. You can pick one up on the Markt, and the ride usually takes about a half hour, with a little stop at the Begijnhof. The price per cart is fixed at €40. In winter blankets are provided as it can be bitterly cold.

BICYCLES

● The best way to get around Brussels is by bicycle, but watch out for traffic. Bicycles are now available to rent from the tourist office in Grand' Place and can be dropped off at several points in the city. You could also try Pro Vélo (✉ Rue de Londres 15, Ixelles ☎ 02 502 7355; www.provelo.org).

● Getting around Bruges by bicycle is great and Damme is only 6.5km (4 miles) away, and Knokke or Zeebrugge less than 21km (13 miles). You can rent bicycles from:
  ● Station Brugge/Bagage (☎ 050 30 23 29).
  ● 't Koffieboontje (✉ Hallestraat 4 ☎ 050 33 80 27; www.adventure-bike-renting.be).
  ● Eric Popelier (✉ 26 Mariastraat ☎ 050 34 32 62; also has tandems and scooters).
  ● Bauhaus Bike Rental (✉ 145 Langestraat ☎ 050 34 10 93; www.bauhaus.be).

● Major rail stations in Belgium sell tickets for train journey and bicycle rental (✉ 02 528 2828).

BUSES, TRAMS AND METRO IN BRUSSELS

● Brussels' metro stations are indicated by a white letter 'M'.
  Line 1A: Roi Baudouin to Hermann Debroux.
  1B: Gare de l'Ouest to Stockel.
  Line 2: Circle line from Simonis (Elisabeth) to Simonis (Leopold II).
  Pré-Métro: from Gare du Nord to Gare du Midi and Albert.

● For information on the metro, trams and buses in Brussels, contact STIB/MIVB ✉ 6th floor, Galerie de la Toison d'Or 20 ☎ 070 23 20 00; www.stib.be.

● One-way tickets are available at metro stations, from bus or tram drivers or at news-agents with the STIB sign. Special tickets are available at metro stations or from the tourist office in Grand' Place. A ticket is valid for one hour on bus, tram or metro. You must get the

ticket validated in the electronic readers on the bus/tram or in the metro station.

BUSES IN BRUGES
● Although this guide gives bus numbers for sights, the heart of the city is small and walkable. However, the efficient bus network makes it easy to explore farther afield.
● Buy tickets on board or from newsstands (in which case you must get them stamped on the bus). A one-day pass (*dagticket*) is available.
● Information line ☎ 0800 13663.
● Up-to-date bus schedules are on display at the Bruges Tourist Office.

TAXIS
● In Brussels, use only official taxis, with a taxi light on the roof. They also have a yellow and blue triangle on the roof. Taxis are metered and can be called or flagged down, but are not allowed to stop if you are less than 100m (110 yards) from a taxi stand. The meter price is per kilometer and is doubled if you travel outside the city (☎ 02 411 41 42 or 02 715 4040).

● In Bruges, taxi stands are on Markt (☎ 050 33 44 44) and at the rail station (☎ 050 38 46 60).

TRAINS
● Brussels has three main stations: Gare du Midi/Zuidstation, Gare Centrale/Centraal Station and Gare du Nord/Noordstation. Two other stations, Schuman and Quartier Léopold, serve the EU institutions and the headquarters of NATO. Bruges has only one station, near the heart of the city.
● Tickets are sold in stations, not on the train. Special offers are available on weekends and for day trips.
● Frequent trains from Brussels run to the outlying areas and from Bruges to the coast.
● Train information: SNCB/NMBS ☎ 02 528 2828; www.belgianrail.be.

NEED TO KNOW GETTING AROUND

Essential Facts

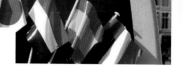

Many Bruges museums (www.museabrugge.be), except some privately owned ones, close on Monday.

The euro is the official currency of Belgium. Bank notes come in denominations of 5, 10, 20, 50, 100, 200 and 500 euros and coins in denominations of 1, 2, 5, 10, 20 and 50 cents and 1 and 2 euros.

LOST/STOLEN PROPERTY

● Report stolen property to the police. For insurance purposes, ask for a certificate of loss.
● Brussels' central police station is at rue du Marché au Charbon 30 (☎ 02 279 7711). Bruges' central police station is at Hauwerstraat 3 (☎ 050 44 88 44).
● The Lost-and-Found office in Brussels is at rue du Frontispice 55 (☎ 02 274 1690). Lost Property offices for public transport are at: Porte de Namur metro station, Brussels ☎ 02 515 2394; Stationplein 5, Bruges ☎ 050 30 23 28.

MAIL

● Stamps are available from post offices and vending machines.
● Brussels' most centrally located post office is at boulevard Anspach 1 (☎ 02 226 9700 🕒 Mon–Fri 8–6, Sat 10.30–4.30).
● Bruges Post Office is at Markt 5 (☎ 022 01 23 45 🕒 Mon–Fri 9–6, Sat 9–3).

MEDICAL TREATMENT

● ▷ 116 for details of the European Health Insurance Card.
● Most doctors speak French and English and can visit if you are too sick to move. Visits must be paid for in cash or by check. The following hospitals provide 24-hour emergency assistance:

MEDICAL TREATMENT IN BRUSSELS

● Cliniques Universitaires ✉ Avenue d'Hippocrate 10, St.-Luc, Woluwe St.-Lambert ☎ 02 764 1111
● Hôpital St-Pierre ✉ Rue Haute 322 ☎ 02 506 7141
● Hôpital Universitaire des Enfants Reine Fabiola (for children) ✉ Avenue Jean Crocq 15, Laeken ☎ 02 477 3311

MEDICAL TREATMENT IN BRUGES

● Akademisch Ziekenhuis Sint-Jan ✉ Ruddershove 10 ☎ 050 45 21 11
● Algemeen Ziekenhuis Sint-Lucas ✉ St.-Lucaslaan 29 ☎ 050 36 91 11

MEDICINES
● Pharmacies (*Pharmacie/Apotheek*), marked with a green cross, open Mon–Fri 9–6. Each displays a list of pharmacies that open outside these hours.

NEWSPAPERS
● Newspapers include the Flemish *De Morgen* and *De Standaard* and the French-language *Le Soir*.

SENSIBLE PRECAUTIONS
● By law, visitors over 21 must carry a passport or ID card at all times.
● Watch out for pickpockets and bag-snatchers, particularly in crowded areas in Brussels and at stations.
● In Brussels, take a taxi at night, rather than the metro, bus or tram.
● Be careful in downtown Brussels, especially the red-light area at Gare du Nord, which can be dangerous at night, and the area near Comte de Flandre metro station, which is known for street crime.

SMOKING
● Smoking is banned in public places and in most restaurants and bars.

TELEPHONES
● Many phone booths accept only prepaid phone cards, available from post offices, super-markets, stations and newsstands.
● International calls are expensive. Rates are slightly lower 8pm–8am and on Sunday.
● The city codes (☎ 02 for Brussels; 050 for Bruges) must be used even when calling from within the city.
● To call the UK from Belgium dial 00 44, then drop the first 0 from the area code. To call Belgium from the UK dial 00 32, then drop the first 0 from the area code.
● To call the US from Belgium dial 001. To call Belgium from the US dial 011 32, then drop the first 0 from the area code.

EMERGENCY TELEPHONE NUMBERS

Ambulance/fire ☎ 100
Police ☎ 101

Brussels' doctors on emergency ☎ 02 479 1818; www.mgbru.be

Bruges' doctors on emergency 🕔 Fri–Mon 8am–8pm ☎ 078 15 15 90

General emergency ☎ 112
24-hour Red Cross ambulance ☎ 105

TOILETS

Public toilets are usually clean. Tip attendants in bigger restaurants and cafés; the amount is posted on the wall.

Language

English is widely understood in Belgium, but if you'd like to try the local language, here are some phrases that may help. Be sure to choose the correct language—if you speak French to a Flemish person, they might be offended. Similarly, if you speak Flemish to a French-speaking *Bruxellois*, they may well reply in French with some disdain.

BASIC VOCABULARY (FRENCH)

Oui/Non	Yes/no
S'il vous plaît	Please
Merci	Thank you
Excusez-moi	Excuse me
Bonjour	Hello
Au revoir	Good-bye
Parlez-vous anglais?	Do you speak English?
Je ne comprends pas	I don't understand
Combien?	How much?
Où est/sont...?	Where is/are...?
Ici/là	Here/there
Tournez à gauche/ droite	Turn left/right
Tout droit	Straight on
Quand?	When?
Aujourd'hui	Today
Hier	Yesterday
Demain	Tomorrow
Combien de temps?	How long?
À quelle heure ouvrez/fermez-vous?	What time do you open/close?
Avez vous...?	Do you have...?
Une chambre simple	A single room
Une chambre double	A double room
Avec salle de bains	With bathroom
Le petit déjeuner	Breakfast
Le déjeuner	Lunch
Le dîner	Dinner
Acceptez-vous des cartes de crédit?	Do you accept credit cards?
J'ai besoin d'un médecin/dentiste	I need a doctor/ dentist
Pouvez-vous m'aider?	Can you help me?
Où est l'hôpital?	Where is the hospital?
Où est le commissariat?	Where is the police station?

NUMBERS (FRENCH)

un	1
deux	2
trois	3
quatre	4
cinq	5
six	6
sept	7
huit	8
neuf	9
dix	10
onze	11
douze	12
treize	13
quatorze	14
quinze	15
seize	16
dix-sept	17
dix-huit	18
dix-neuf	19
vingt	20

CONVERSATION (FLEMISH)

Ja/neen	Yes/no
Alstublieft	Please
Dank u	Thank you
Excuseer	Excuse me
Hallo	Hello
Goedemorgen	Good morning
Goedenavond	Good evening
Tot ziens	Good-bye
Spreekt u Engels?	Do you speak English?
Ik begrijp u niet	I don't understand

USEFUL QUESTIONS (FLEMISH)

Hoeveel?	How much?
Waar is/ zijn…?	Where is/are…?
Wanneer?	When?
Hoelang?	How long?
Wanneer is het open/ gesloten?	At what time do you open/close?
Heeft u…?	Do you have…?
Hoeveel kost dit?	How much is this?
Aanvaard u een kredietkaart?	Do you take credit cards?
Kunt u mij helpen?	Can you help me?
Waar is het ziekenhuis/politie kantoor?	Where is the hospital/police station?

WORDS AND PHRASES (FLEMISH)

Hier	Here
Daar	There
Sla rechts af	Turn right
Sla links af	Turn left
Rechtdoor	Straight
Een enkele kamer	A single room
Een dubbele kamer	A double room
Met/zonder badkamer	With/without a bathroom
Ik heb een dokter/ tandarts nodig	I need a doctor/ dentist

NUMBERS (FLEMISH)

een	1
twee	2
drie	3
vier	4
vijf	5
zes	6
zeven	7
acht	8
negen	9
tien	10
elf	11
twaalf	12
dertien	13
veertien	14
vijftien	15
zestien	16
zeventien	17
achttien	18
negentien	19
twintig	20
een en twintig	21
dertig	30
veertig	40
vijftig	50
zestig	60
zeventig	70
tachtig	80
negentig	90
honderd	100
duizend	1,000

WHEN? (FLEMISH)

Vandaag	Today
Gisteren	Yesterday
Morgen	Tomorrow
Ontbijt	Breakfast
Lunch	Lunch
Diner/ avondeten	Dinner

Timeline

EARLY DAYS

- Brocsella (Brussels) was first mentioned in AD695 on the trade route between Cologne and Flanders.
- In 979, Charles, Duke of Lorraine, moved to St.-Géry (central Brussels), founding the city.
- In 1459 Philip the Good, having inherited Flanders and Burgundy, brought Brabant and Holland under his control and settled in Brussels.

BRUSSELS

1515 Charles V, soon to be Holy Roman Emperor and King of Spain and the Netherlands, arrives in the city and rules his empire from here until he abdicates in 1555.

1568 A revolt begins that leads to the independence of the United Provinces of the Netherlands from Spain, but not of present-day Belgium, which becomes known as the Spanish Netherlands.

1695 French forces attack Brussels, destroying 4,000 buildings.

1713–94 Brussels is capital of the Austrian Netherlands, under Habsburg rule.

1795 Brussels is under French rule.

1815 Brussels reverts to the Dutch, after Napoleon Bonaparte's defeat at Waterloo.

1830 The Belgian Revolution leads to independence in January 1831.

1957 Brussels becomes the HQ of the EEC.

2002 Euro notes and coins are introduced.

2009 Magritte Museum opens.

2013 King Albert II abdicates in July in favor of his son Philippe.

From left to right: Napoleon; a map showing the positions of the British and French armies at the Battle of Waterloo; Europe Day celebrations in Brussels; Charles V; a man in medieval dress

BRUGES

AD800–900 Bryggja is established, named for the Norse for "harbor."

1127 The first walls go up around Bruges.

1302 Flemish craftsmen and peasants defeat a French army at the Battle of the Golden Spurs.

1488 An uprising against the Habsburg Archduke Maximilian leads to his kidnap and three months' detention in Bruges. The reprisals against the Bruges burghers begin the steady decline of the city when Maximilian becomes emperor in 1493.

1898 Flemish is officially recognized as the country's joint language with French.

2000 Bruges becomes a UNESCO World Heritage Site.

2002 The Concertgebouw opens, putting Bruges at the forefront of Flanders' cultural life.

2007 Filming begins of the British movie *In Bruges*, by Martin McDonagh. The plot revolves around two hit men who end up in the city.

2013 Bruges' mayor, Renaat Landuyt, cautions against Bruges becoming a "film studio" as the success of *In Bruges* draws increasing numbers of film crews to the city.

TRADING SUCCESS

By the early 14th century Bruges had become one of the world's great trading cities. In 1384 Philip the Bold, Duke of Burgundy, inherited Flanders and ushered in a period of prosperity and great cultural and political changes. However, the city began to decline when Maximilian became emperor in 1493. In 1516 Genoese and Florentine traders, who had set up business ventures in Bruges under a treaty of 1395, moved to Antwerp. A further difficulty arose in 1550, when Bruges lost access to the sea, with the silting up of the inlet that is now known as the Zwin.

Index

A

accommodations 18, 107–112
  Bruges 108, 109, 111, 112
  Brussels 108–112
airports 116–117
antiques 12, 16
  Bruges 89
  Brussels 40, 41, 57
Antwerp 103
Army Museum 51
art nouveau 16, 24, 32, 50,
  52–53, 56, 57
Atomium 98–99
Autoworld 51
avenue Louise 54

B

bars and clubs 13, 15
  Bruges 90
  Brussels 42, 43, 59
Basiliek van het Heilig-
  Bloed 83
Basilique National du Sacré-
  Coeur 102
beers and breweries 11, 57,
  83, 91
Begijnhof 9, 66–67
BELvue Museum 36
bicycling 56, 118
Bois de la Cambre 54
bookshops 12
  Bruges 89
  Brussels 40, 41, 57
Boudewijn Seapark 18, 102
Bourse 33
BOZAR 35
Brangwyn Museum 74
Brouwerij de Halve Maan 83
Bruges 4, 5, 63–92
  accommodations 108, 109,
    111, 112
  entertainment and nightlife
    90
  map 64–65
  one-day itinerary 7
  restaurants 91–92
  shopping 88–89
  sights 66–86
  walk 87
Bruparck 102
Brussels 4, 5
  accommodations 108–112
  one-day itinerary 6
  see also Central Brussels;
    South Brussels
Brussels Card 33
Burg 9, 68–69
buses 117, 119

C

canal cruise 9, 70
cathedrals and churches
  Basiliek van het Heilig-Bloed
    83
  Basilique Nationale du
    Sacré-Coeur 102
  Cathédrale des Sts. Michel
    et Gudule 35
  Église Notre Dame du
    Sablon 34
  Église St.-Jacques-sur-
    Coudenberg 33
  Église St.-Nicolas 36
  Jeruzalemkerk 84–85
  Kathedraal St.-Salvator
    8, 75
  Onze-Lieve-Vrouwekerk
    (Bruges) 8, 78–79
  Onze-Lieve-Vrouwekerk
    (Damme) 96–97
  St.-Jakobskerk 86
  Sint-Walburgakerk 86
Centenary Stadium 98, 99
Central Brussels 20–46
  entertainment and nightlife
    42–43
  map 22–23
  restaurants 44–46
  shopping 40–41
  sights 24–37
  walk 38
La Centrale Électrique/de
  Elektriciteitscentrale 35–36
Centre Belge de la Bande
  Dessinée 8, 16, 24
children's activities 18
chocolate 10, 12, 17, 41,
  88, 89
Choco-Story (Bruges) 8, 17, 71
cinema
  Bruges 90
  Brussels 42, 43, 59
climate and seasons 114
Collégiale des Sts.-Pierre et
  Guidon 54
Concertgebouw 18, 83–84, 90
cookies 10
crime and personal safety 121
cultural venues
  Bruges 90
  Brussels 42, 43

D

Damme 8, 96–97
dance, contemporary 59
Diamantmuseum 84
disabilities, visitors with 117

E

eating out 14–15
  Belgian cuisine 14
  vegetarian food 14, 62
  see also restaurants
Église Notre Dame du Sablon
  34
Église St.-Jacques-sur-
  Coudenberg 33
Église St.-Nicolas 36
emergencies 121
entertainment and nightlife 13
  Bruges 90
  Central Brussels 42–43
  South Brussels 59
European Centre for
  Contemporary Art 35–36
European Parliament 54
European Union 5, 54
excursions
  Antwerp 103
  Ghent 103
  Ieper (Ypres) 105
  Ostend 105
  Walibi 106
  Waterloo 106

F

fashion shopping 10, 11, 12
  Bruges 88
  Brussels 41, 57, 58
ferry services 117
festivals and events 114
Film Museum 35, 43
food shopping 10–11, 12
  Bruges 88, 89
  Brussels 40–41, 57, 58

G

gay scene 43, 90
Ghent 103
Grand' Place 8, 16, 17, 26–27
Groeninge Museum 8, 17,
  72–73
Gruuthuse Museum 8, 74

H

Heysel 8, 98–99
history 124–125
Horta, Victor 24, 35, 51, 52–53
Hôtel de Ville 9, 25
hotels 18, 107–112

I

Ieper (Ypres) 105
insurance 116
Internet access 115
Ixelles 54

J
Jan van Eyckplein 84
Jardin Botanique Meise
   100–101
Jeruzalemkerk 84–85

K
Kathedraal St.-Salvator 8, 75
Koningin Astridpark 85

L
lace 11, 88, 89
Laeken 102
language 4, 122–123
lost property 120

M
Maison Cauchie 50
Manneken-Pis 9, 28
Marché du Midi 55
markets
   Bruges 86
   Brussels 16, 36, 55, 58
Markt 8, 76–77
Les Marolles 36–37
medical treatment 120, 121
Memling, Hans 81, 84
metro (Brussels) 118–119
Meunier, Constantin 55
Minnewater 85
Modern Art, Museum of 9, 29
money 120
museums
   Autoworld 51
   BELvue Museum 36
   Brangwyn Museum 74
   Centre Belge de la Bande
      Dessinée 8, 16, 24
   Choco-Story (Bruges)
      8, 17, 71
   Comic Strip Museum
      8, 16, 24
   Diamantmuseum 84
   Film Museum 35, 43
   Groeninge Museum 8, 17,
      72–73
   Gruuthuse Museum 8, 74
   Musée d'Art Ancien 9, 17,
      30–31
   Musée d'Art Moderne 9, 29
   Musée BELvue 36
   Musée d'Ixelles 55
   Musée du Cinema 35, 43
   Musée du Cinquantenaire 51
   Musée Constantin Meunier
      55
   Musée David et Alice van
      Buuren 55

Musée des Instruments de
   Musique 9, 16, 32
Musée Royal de l'Armée et
   d'Histoire Militaire 51
Musée Horta 9, 16, 52–53
Musée de la Ville de Bruxelles
   37
Museum Onze-Lieve-
   Vrouwter Potterie 85
Museum voor Volkskunde
   85–86
St.-Janshospitaal en Memling
   Museum 8, 80–81
music venues 18
   Bruges 90
   Brussels 42, 43, 59

N
newspapers 121

O
Old England Building 32
Onze-Lieve-Vrouwekerk
   (Bruges) 8, 78–79
Onze-Lieve-Vrouwekerk
   (Damme) 96–97
opera 18, 37
Ostend 105

P
Landhuis van het Brugse
   Vrije 69
Palais de Justice 37
Palais Royal 33
Parc du Cinquantenaire
   9, 50–51
passports and visas 117
pharmacies 121
place Royale 9, 33
place Ste.-Catherine 37
place St.-Géry 37
police 120, 121
post offices 120
public transport 118–119

R
restaurants 15, 17
   Bruges 91–92
   Central Brussels 44–46
   South Brussels 60–62
Royal Greenhouses 102

S
Le Sablon 9, 34
St.-Jakobskerk 86
St.-Janshospitaal en Memling
   Museum 8, 80–81
St.-Janshuismolen 86

Serres Royales 102
shopping 10–12, 16
   Bruges 11, 12, 88–89
   Brussels 40–41, 57–58
Sint-Walburgakerk 86
South Brussels 47–62
   bicycle tour 56
   entertainment and nightlife
      59
   map 48–49
   restaurants 60–62
   shopping 57–58
   sights 50–55
stamp shops 40
Stock Exchange 35
student travelers 119

T
taxis 119
telephones 121
theater
   Bruges 90
   Brussels 42, 43, 59
Théâtre Royal de la Monnaie
   18, 37
theme parks 18, 102, 106
ticket outlets 13, 42
time differences 114
Tintin 11, 24, 40, 89
toilets 121
tourist information 115
Town Hall (Bruges) 69
Town Hall (Brussels) 9, 25
train travel 117, 119

V
De Vesten en Poorten 8, 82
Vismarkt 86

W
Walibi 18, 106
walks
   Bruges 87
   Central Brussels 38
Waterloo 106
websites 115
windmills 86

Z
De Zeven Torentjes 102

INDEX

Brussels & Bruges 25 Best

WRITTEN BY Anthony Sattin and Sylvie Franquet
UPDATED BY Des Hannigan
SERIES EDITOR Clare Ashton
COVER DESIGN Chie Ushio, Yuko Inagaki
DESIGN WORK Tracey Freestone
IMAGE RETOUCHING AND REPRO Jacqueline Street-Elkayam

Published in the United Kingdom by AA Publishing

ISBN 978-1-1018-7943-6

FIFTH EDITION

All details in this book are based on information supplied to us at press time. Always confirm information when it matters, especially if you're making a detour to visit a specific place. Fodor's expressly disclaims any liability, loss, or risk, personal or otherwise, that is incurred as a consequence of the use of any of the contents of this book.

SPECIAL SALES
This book is available for special discounts for bulk purchases for sales promotions or premiums. For more information, email specialmarkets@randomhouse.com.

Color separation by AA Digital Department
Printed and bound by Leo Paper Products, China

10 9 8 7 6 5 4 3 2 1

A05314
Maps in this title produced from mapping © MAIRDUMONT / Falk Verlag 2012 and data from openstreetmap.org © OpenStreetMap contributors
Transport map © Communicarta Ltd, UK

The Automobile Association would like to thank the following photographers, companies and picture libraries for their assistance in the preparation of this book.

2 AA/A Kouprianoff; **3** AA/A Kouprianoff; **4t** AA/A Kouprianoff; **4c** AA/A Kouprianoff; **5t** AA/A Kouprianoff; **5c** AA/A Kouprianoff; **6t** AA/A Kouprianoff; **6cl** AA/A Kouprianoff; **6c** AA/A Kouprianoff; **6cr** AA/A Kouprianoff; **6bl** AA/A Kouprianoff; **6bc** AA/A Kouprianoff; **6br** AA/A Kouprianoff; **7t** AA/A Kouprianoff; **7cl** AA/A Kouprianoff; **7c** AA/A Kouprianoff; **7cr** AA/A Kouprianoff; **7bl** AA/A Kouprianoff; **7bc** AA/A Kouprianoff; **7br** AA/A Kouprianoff; **8** AA/A Kouprianoff; **9** AA/A Kouprianoff; **10t** AA/A Kouprianoff; **10ct** AA/A Kouprianoff; **10c** AA/A Kouprianoff; **10/11cb** AA/A Kouprianoff; **10/11b** AA/A Kouprianoff; **11t** AA/A Kouprianoff; **11ct** AA/A Kouprianoff; **11c** AA/A Kouprianoff; **12** AA/A Kouprianoff; **13t** AA/A Kouprianoff; **13ct** AA/A Kouprianoff; **13c** Digital Vision; **13cb** AA/A Kouprianoff; **13b** AA/A Kouprianoff; **14t** AA/A Kouprianoff; **14ct** AA/A Kouprianoff; **14c** AA/A Kouprianoff; **14cb** AA/A Kouprianoff; **14b** AA/A Kouprianoff; **15t** AA/A Kouprianoff; **15b** AA/A Kouprianoff; **16t** AA/A Kouprianoff; **16ct** AA/A Kouprianoff; **16c** AA/A Kouprianoff; **16cb** AA/A Kouprianoff; **16b** AA/A Kouprianoff; **17t** AA/A Kouprianoff; **17ct** AA/A Kouprianoff; **17c** AA/A Kouprianoff; **17cb** AA/A Kouprianoff; **17b** Hemis/Alamy; **18t** AA/A Kouprianoff; **18ct** Stockbyte; **18c** AA/A Kouprianoff; **18cb** Courtesy of Six Flags Belgium; **18b** Courtesy of Six Flags Belgium; **19t** AA/A Kouprianoff; **19ct** AA/A Kouprianoff; **19cb** AA/A Kouprianoff; **19b** AA/A Kouprianoff; **20/21** AA/A Kouprianoff; **24l** AA; **24r** AA/A Kouprianoff; **25l** AA/A Kouprianoff; **25r** AA/A Kouprianoff; **26l** AA/A Kouprianoff; **26tr** AA/A Kouprianoff; **26/27** AA/A Kouprianoff; **27t** AA; **27cl** AA/A Kouprianoff; **27cr** AA/A Kouprianoff; **28l** AA/A Kouprianoff; **28c** AA; **28r** AA/A Kouprianoff; **29l** AA/A Kouprianoff; **29c** AA/A Kouprianoff; **29r** AA/A Kouprianoff; **30** Courtesy of Musee d'Art Ancien; **30/31** Courtesy of Musee d'Art Ancien; **31** Courtesy of Musee d'Art Ancien Puits de Limiere; **32l** AA/A Kouprianoff; **32r** AA/A Kouprianoff; **33l** AA/A Kouprianoff; **33r** AA/A Kouprianoff; **34l** AA/A Kouprianoff; **34r** AA/A Kouprianoff; **35t** AA/A Kouprianoff; **35bl** AA/A Kouprianoff; **35br** AA/A Kouprianoff; **36t** AA/A Kouprianoff; **36bl** AA/A Kouprianoff; **36br** AA/A Kouprianoff; **37t** AA/A Kouprianoff; **37b** AA/A Kouprianoff; **38** AA/A Kouprianoff; **39** AA/A Kouprianoff; **40** Photodisc; **41** AA/A Kouprianoff; **42** Photodisc; **43** Photodisc; **44** AA/A Kouprianoff; **45** AA/C Sawyer; **46** AA/A Kouprianoff; **47** AA/A Kouprianoff; **50t** AA/A Kouprianoff; **50cl** AA/A Kouprianoff; **50cr** AA/A Kouprianoff; **51t** AA/A Kouprianoff; **50/51** AA/A Kouprianoff; **51cr** AA/A Kouprianoff; **52** © Paul Cornelissen/Alamy; **52/53** © LOOK Die Bildagentur der Fotografen GmbH/Alamy; **54t** AA/A Kouprianoff; **54b** AA/A Kouprianoff; **55t** AA/A Kouprianoff; **55b** AA/A Kouprianoff; **56** AA/A Kouprianoff; **57** AA/A Kouprianoff; **58** AA/A Kouprianoff; **59** Brand X Pics; **60** AA/T Souter; **61** AA/A Kouprianoff; **62** AA/A Kouprianoff; **63** AA/A Kouprianoff; **66** AA/A Kouprianoff; **66/67** AA/A Kouprianoff; **68tl** AA/A Kouprianoff; **68cl** AA/A Kouprianoff; **68/69** AA/A Kouprianoff; **68cr** AA/A Kouprianoff; **69cl** AA/A Kouprianoff; **69r** AA/A Kouprianoff; **70l** AA/A Kouprianoff; **70r** AA/A Kouprianoff; **71l** Choco-Story Chocolate Museum; **71c** Choco-Story Chocolate Museum; **71r** Choco-Story Chocolate Museum; **72** AA/A Kouprianoff; **72/73** AA/A Kouprianoff; **74l** AA/A Kouprianoff; **74r** AA; **75l** AA/A Kouprianoff; **75r** AA/A Kouprianoff; **76l** AA/A Kouprianoff; **76tr** AA/A Kouprianoff; **76cr** AA/A Kouprianoff; **77t** AA/A Kouprianoff; **77cl** AA/A Kouprianoff; **77cr** AA/A Kouprianoff; **78/79** AA/A Kouprianoff; **79** AA/A Kouprianoff; **80** Memling Museum; **80/81** Memling Museum; **82** AA/A Kouprianoff; **83t** AA/A Kouprianoff; **83bl** AA/A Kouprianoff; **83br** AA/A Kouprianoff; **84t** AA/A Kouprianoff; **84b** AA/A Kouprianoff; **85t** AA/A Kouprianoff; **85b** Alamy (©Rough Guides); **86t** AA/A Kouprianoff; **86b** Alamy (©Andrew Critchell); **87** AA/A Kouprianoff; **88** AA/A Kouprianoff; **89** AA/A Kouprianoff; **90** Digital Vision; **91** AA/A Kouprianoff; **92** AA/A Kouprianoff; **93** AA/A Kouprianoff; **96** AA/A Kouprianoff; **96/97** AA/A Kouprianoff; **98l** AA/A Kouprianoff; **98/99** AA/A Kouprianoff; **99** AA/A Kouprianoff; **100t** Arterra Picture Library/Alamy; **100cl** Pete M. Wilson/Alamy; **100cr** Arterra Picture Library/Alamy; **101** Chris Howes/Wild Places Photography/Alamy; **102t** AA/A Kouprianoff; **102bl** AA/A Kouprianoff; **102br** AA/A Kouprianoff; **103t** AA/A Kouprianoff; **103bl** AA/A Kouprianoff; **103bc** AA/A Kouprianoff; **103br** AA/A Kouprianoff; **104** AA/A Kouprianoff; **105t** AA/A Kouprianoff; **105bl** AA/A Kouprianoff; **105br** AA/A Kouprianoff; **106t** AA/A Kouprianoff; **106bl** AA/A Kouprianoff; **106br** AA/A Kouprianoff; **107** AA/A Kouprianoff; **108t** AA/C Sawyer; **108ct** Photodisc; **108c** AA/A Kouprianoff; **108cb** Photodisc; **108b** Photodisc; **109–112** AA/C Sawyer; **113** AA/A Kouprianoff; **114–117** AA/A Kouprianoff; **116b** AA/A Kouprianoff; **118–125** AA/A Kouprianoff; **122c** AA/A Kouprianoff; **124bl** AA; **124bc** AA/A Kouprianoff; **124/125** AA/A Kouprianoff; **125bc** AA; **125br** AA/A Kouprianoff

Titles in the Series

- Amsterdam
- Bangkok
- Barcelona
- Boston
- Brussels and Bruges
- Budapest
- Chicago
- Dubai
- Dublin
- Edinburgh
- Florence
- Hong Kong
- Istanbul
- Krakow
- Las Vegas
- Lisbon
- London
- Madrid
- Melbourne
- Milan
- Montréal
- Munich
- New York City
- Orlando
- Paris
- Rome
- San Francisco
- Seattle
- Shanghai
- Singapore
- Sydney
- Tokyo
- Toronto
- Venice
- Vienna
- Washington, D.C.